TO FIGHT BETTER

'. . . *baffled to fight better*'
– Robert Browning

TO FIGHT BETTER

A biography of
J Oswald Sanders

Ron and Gwen Roberts

HIGHLAND BOOKS
OVERSEAS MISSIONARY FELLOWSHIP

ISBN 0 946616 58 2

Cover design: Graham Turner, Spectra Graphics

Photoset by Rowland Phototypesetting Ltd
Bury St Edmunds, Suffolk
Printed in Great Britain for
HIGHLAND BOOKS
Broadway House, The Broadway
Crowborough, East Sussex TN6 1HQ
by Richard Clay Ltd, Bungay, Suffolk.

Contents

For 'Madge'

in memory of
her father

Acknowledgements

This book could not have been written without the generous assistance of many who contributed a varied store of recollections and experiences concerning the life of J O Sanders.

My husband was fascinated by the challenge of weaving each of these different strands into a tapestry that would display something of the many-hued grace of God at work in a human life.

Then suddenly, and without warning one summer morning, a massive heart attack opened the gate through which Ron passed into the company of those whose endless theme is 'Worthy the Lamb!'

The loose strands and the challenge of that tapestry remained. Finally it seemed right that I should try to finish the task. Now on Ron's behalf, and my own, I want to thank all who contributed those strands:

Mrs Peggy Adair, Miss Barbara Allison, Rev N Andersen, Miss Jean Anderson, Mr G A Ardrey, Dr D W Bacon, Mr George Bremner, Rev Will Bruce, Mr Leonard Buck, Mrs Alison Butler, Mr Ralph Davis, Dr Diana Dunn, Mr Gerald Ford, Mrs Daphne Gibson, Mr Don Goldney, the late Mr D V Gonden, Mrs Naomi Grant, Miss Ruth Grey, Dr M C Griffiths, Mr Russell Grigg, Mr Andrew Johnston, Mr F Keeble, Rev I Kemp, the late Rev H Knight, Mrs Nancy Knight, the late Dr John Laird, Mr Arnold Lea, Mr Norman and Mrs Amy McIntosh, the late Mr W Michell, Mrs Amy Moore, Dr Leon Morris, Mr Wheeler Paterson, Mr T Pryde, Mr E Peipman, Mrs O Pound, Mrs D Quinn, Miss Beth Roose, Mr L Rushbrook, Mr D Shortt, Mr Leonard Street, Mrs Lois Strong, Miss Isabel Taylor, Dr Paul White.

My special thanks go to Mrs Rosemary Robertson for careful typing of the manuscript and to Mrs Ann Rogers and my daughter, Margaret Rumbold, for helpful criticism of the text.

It is impossible to express the debt I owe to Keith and Val Butler who from the outset not only gave constant prayer support themselves but also kept informed a wider group of interested friends. In a very real sense this book belongs to all of you who prayed.

Finally I must thank Mrs Marjorie Rumbold for cheerful encouragement through the months of writing.

Gwen Roberts
Sydney, Australia

About this Book

'I'm not going to write it!'

We were clearing away the breakfast dishes, and once again my husband had been urging 'J O' to write his autobiography.

'*Why* won't you write it?'

'I've made too many mistakes, and I've made up my mind. *I'm not going to write it.*' And then, '*You* write it!'

There was a stunned silence; the idea was unthinkable.

But it wouldn't go away. Over the weeks that followed it returned again and again, until at last it was faced: if God was in it, it *could* be possible.

There were no diaries and few letters, but 'J O' was generous with his time and his amazing memory. When friends heard of the possibility, they were enthusiastic in their support. Gradually there emerged the astounding picture of a man who, while appearing to stride tall and serene through all the affairs of life, often suffered the agonies of a sense of inadequacy; a man who, in spite of a nagging sense of inferiority, learned to count on a God who was great enough to see him through.

This is his story.

Foreword

I have been asked by the author to write a foreword to this book – not an easy task for its subject!

It is only the conviction that the experience of God's goodness and guidance in one's life are a trust to be shared with other members of the family of God for their encouragement or warning, that has led me to consent to this biography being written.

Ron Roberts had a long association with CIM/OMF. In 1941 he sailed for China where he later married Gwen. In 1953 he headed up the Mission's rapidly-growing Literature Programme in Hong Kong, until he was appointed Home Director for Australia in 1971 – a post he filled with distinction for ten years. For thirty of those years I had increasing association and friendship with Ron and Gwen.

Ron's sudden homecall when the book was less than half-written was a shock to us all, and it seemed to be the end of the project. But Gwen has bravely stepped into the breach and, from material Ron had collected, has completed the story.

The facts are all there, but I feel that their interpretation has been over-generous. I am conscious of being a very ordinary person with only modest gifts, but God has been pleased to use these gifts beyond my dreaming, insofar as I have yielded them to him. As I grow older the imperfections of my service become painfully clear, and that, in turn, makes me realise that for any blessing that has resulted, the glory is His, not mine.

I believe in the sovereignty of God in a human life, and that it is God's sovereignty, grace and patience that have brought me thus far. For example, when in India, I went to speak to the all-Indian staff of Trans-world Radio. The manager met me with: 'I never expected to meet you in the flesh. I have prayed for you every day for fifteen years!' God had sovereignly laid me on his heart. And I have been blessed with many such faithful prayer partners.

If this story of an ordinary and obscure youth can encourage other ordinary people to yield their lives to Christ's control, even if their following is not as perfect as they would wish, the book will have served its purpose.

J Oswald Sanders
Auckland, New Zealand

INADEQUATE

It was May 1954 and Oswald Sanders sat staring in disbelief at a letter in his hand.

For nearly three years, the China Inland Mission Overseas Missionary Fellowship had been operating without a General Director, and he had been wondering whether the council that had met recently in Singapore had come any nearer to resolving the problem of the Mission's leadership. They had!

The letter, from Mr Arnold Lea, conveyed the council's unanimous invitation to Oswald Sanders to become the Mission's new General Director!

He could not take it in. He felt sure that they were making a mistake. He knew he lacked the background that he would consider desirable for one in such a position. He came from a simple, godly home and while he had had an excellent education at the Southland Boys' High School and some legal training, he lacked academic qualifications and he had had no overseas missionary experience whatever. Besides which he did not want the position; he was unwilling to face the cost involved. But above all, he felt totally inadequate for the task. Many times before, during his fifty-two years, he had experienced that sense of inadequacy, but never more so than on that occasion.

1

A Twig is Bent

Oswald's father, Alfred Sanders, was a real Welshman, with all the Welshman's warmth of temperament, love of music and feeling for words. But before his birth in 1862 his parents had moved from Wales to London, where they established a family business manufacturing the artificial flowers so popular in Victorian homes. The business flourished, especially after they secured the right to display the coveted sign, 'Suppliers to Her Majesty Queen Victoria.' Nevertheless in 1874 Alfred's father, lured by prospects of life in the colonies, sold up the business and took his family to settle in Dunedin, a thriving young city far down the east coast of the South Island of New Zealand.

As with many new settlers, the high hopes with which they had left Britain suffered serious setbacks. Capital was invested in real estate that failed to sell; other funds were lost when the local bank failed. Then followed the familiar story of 'new chums', devoid of any knowledge of farming, committing themselves to a farm. Yet somehow they survived, and young Alfred had learned a good deal about farming before he secured a position as accountant with The University Booksellers in Dunedin.

Always a great reader, the atmosphere of The University Booksellers deepened Alfred's interest in books, and he became something of an authority on Christian literature. A natural corollary was his love for, and extensive knowledge of, words, and in later years his children seldom bothered to consult the dictionary; it was much easier to ask their father!

It was in Dunedin that Alfred met and married Margaret Menzies Miller, whose parents had come to Dunedin from Scotland, leaving their tea business for the bright prospects in New Zealand. Before emigrating they had been influenced by the Keswick Movement, and Margaret, who was born in Dunedin, retained vivid memories of her father spending time alone with God early in the mornings before going off to business. Deeply impressed on her memory was the sight of him pacing the drawing room, quietly singing:

> Take my life and let it be
> Consecrated, Lord, to thee.

Alfred was a short, stocky, dark-haired man of happy, genial disposition but shy and sensitive, with little drive or ambition. Apart from his wife and family, the three loves of his life were books, music and, pre-eminently, the Lord Jesus Christ.

The golden-haired Margaret Sanders was taller than her husband. But the main contrast between them was temperamental for she was a vigorous, dynamic woman, and his lack of drive and easy-going nature held potential for friction between them. Although she did not share his love of books she certainly matched his love of music, and they were completely at one in their Christian convictions.

Some time after their marriage they joined a semi-Brethren group. It was a remarkable assembly. No less than eleven of the elders knew one or other of the original languages of the Bible, and there was a remarkably broad spread of inter-denominational interest and missionary concern. This greatly enlarged the Christian sympathies of the young couple, and all through their lives this wide vision of God's purposes in the world continued. The assembly choir was outstanding, helping to draw some 2,000 people to the Sunday evening gospel services. Husband and wife both sang in the choir, Alfred's fine tenor voice often being heard in solo parts.

Two children were born to them in Dunedin: Alexander Alfred, always known as 'Sandy', followed two years later by Marguerite Amy, generally called 'Rita'. Some four years later a major upheaval came to the young family when Alfred secured the position of accountant of the Invercargill branch of Ross and Glendinning, a large soft goods manufacturing company.

The city of Invercargill is flat, windswept and cold, but as the centre of the most prosperous farming area of New Zealand it has considerable importance and wealth. A large proportion of the early pioneers were Scottish Presbyterians and there is still a pronounced burr in the speech of many people in the region. With the nostalgia common to settlers everywhere, they named the main streets of the new city after Scottish rivers: Clyde, Tay, Dee and, of course, Forth. More importantly, those Presbyterian settlers left a deep mark on the spiritual life of the area.

The city lies below the forty-six-degree line of latitude. Residents commonly claim, 'This is the southernmost city in the world. The next stop is the south pole.' Indeed, the nearby port of Bluff, at the very tip of the South Island, was for many years the jumping-off point for most Antarctic voyages.

But Invercargill was no backwater. Its port was one of the busiest in the country, handling overseas as well as coastal shipping. Many important visitors from all over the world included the city in their itineraries. Thus in 1902 came the famous preacher, Bible teacher and author, Dr Rueben A Torrey, at that time the super-intendent of the Moody Bible Institute in Chicago. Concluding an evangelistic tour of New Zealand, before going on to Australia, Asia and Europe, he was to speak at just one meeting in the city. The Sanders family had just recently arrived, and when Margaret heard about the meeting she resolved to be there. But there was a problem. She was in an advanced stage of pregnancy and the social conventions of the day frowned upon ladies appearing in public at such a time. Margaret, however, was determined, and finally persuaded Alfred to hire a hansom cab and off they went, finding a seat at the back of the hall. Just one week later she gave birth to their third and last child, John Oswald Sanders. The date was 17 October, 1902.

From their earliest days the three children enjoyed a happy, loving, Christian home. Books, music, laughter and genuine piety formed the very elements of their family life. In the evenings the family gathered around Margaret at the organ, singing hymn after hymn. Some nights Alfred, never far from a book, would choose to stay reading in his chair. But he had an extraordinary capacity to sing along with the family, almost uncon-sciously, while continuing to concentrate on his reading. Then the children would search for some obscure hymn, hoping to stump their father. But it was no good; choose what they would he continued to sing with them, fault-less in both words and music. Hospitality also charac-terised the home. Many visiting missionaries and other Christian workers were entertained, each one helping to extend the children's perspectives.

Margaret was a particularly zealous and effective Christian worker, and many a sailor idly wandering the streets of the city heard and believed the gospel through her. Alfred was not a fluent speaker, but he was certainly a good and diligent witness to the Lord Jesus. Unfortunately they did not find in Invercargill a group of fellow Christians comparable to the assembly they had enjoyed so much in Dunedin. Here their wide interests and sympathies were not shared, and at times even the peace-loving Alfred found himself obliged to protest against narrow views and stuffy attitudes.

The three children got along well with each other. Alexander, known to the other two as 'Lex', was six years older than Oswald. He was brilliant. He could skim rapidly through a book and remember what he had read, so he handled his school-work effortlessly. More important, as far as Rita and Oswald were concerned, was his lively imagination and Celtic gift for story-telling. Every night for years, he regaled the other two with a fresh episode of a long-running story he made up as he went along. 'There was never any problem about getting us to go to bed,' Oswald recalls.

With such a happy, wholesome family life it seems surprising that as a small boy Oswald was painfully shy. One day, when he was about ten, a friend brought her two small daughters with her when she called on Margaret. Today those two girls, and Oswald, remember that all through the visit he hid behind a cupboard! He inherited this shyness from his father, along with his dark hair, his fun-loving spirit and his love of books and words. The principal legacy from Margaret was without doubt her driving energy. His love of music must have been a joint legacy.

Neither parent could bequeath their Christian faith, but they were both diligent in pointing the way and in providing living evidence of its truth. Finally the matter was settled for Oswald as well as Rita on 11 March, 1911, when Alfred took them to hear a visiting evangelist with the unmistakably American name of John Quincey

Adams Henry. Oswald was then only eight-and-a-half, but he says, 'I had a real sense of spiritual need, and I made a genuine response to the invitation to receive Christ as my Saviour.' Rita and he both dated their conversion from that night. God had actually prepared the boy for this experience by some remarkable meetings held in the home three or four years earlier.

His parents regularly took part in an open-air meeting every Sunday night after the gospel service. 'They were not a particularly praying lot,' Oswald recalls, but one evening, after the meeting, they spontaneously decided to go to the Sanders' home for prayer. They may not have known much about praying, but they were quick learners. They prayed until midnight! And every night for the next three months they came and prayed until midnight and beyond, mingling prayer and confession with joyous songs of praise. God was truly in their midst and sovereignly in control.

Young Oswald, in bed in the next room, would generally lie awake during the early part of the meeting, and although he could not understand it, somehow he sensed a great wonder – God was in his home! Scripture passages quoted, some repeated night after night, impressed themselves on his young mind with an amazing clarity that has never dimmed over the years. It was listening to those meetings that developed in him 'a sensitivity to the spiritual' that was to influence his whole life and ministry.

Somewhere round about that time a shadow fell across the home that had known almost unbroken sunshine. From some mysterious, never-determined cause, Margaret suffered a baffling change of personality. Outwardly, life went on much as before; there were still plenty of happy times, especially with Rita, and the bond with his father remained unbroken. But some vital element was lost, and family life was never quite the same again. Oswald, already struggling with acute shyness, responded by learning to suppress his emotions and to avoid disappointment by concealing desire. He began to adopt an air of aloofness as a cover for his shyness. The mask became fixed, and for most of his life all but his intimates have seen him as a person who always appeared to be in command of the situation; a person not easy to know.

From the beginning of school-days he had greatly enjoyed holidays on an uncle's farm some eighty miles from Invercargill. Now the appeal was even greater. His uncle and aunt were understanding and kind, and he relaxed and revelled in the rural life. It was no hardship to rise at 4 am to milk the cows and check the rabbit traps. His uncle had a horse that had been used for racing. One day when Oswald was riding this horse he had worked him up to an exciting gallop when he saw that they were rapidly nearing a gate. The horse disregarded all attempts to pull him up. Oswald, concluding that he was going to jump the gate, had prepared himself for the leap when, at the last moment, the horse stopped in his tracks and sent Oswald over his head and over the gate. Happily, the fall broke no bones. Nor did it shatter his love affair with the farm. Indeed, until he was fifteen he was quite sure that this was going to be his career. That year the winter was particularly severe. One day, mud to the knees, and hands all but frozen from pulling turnips for the cattle, he decided that his future must lie elsewhere.

One of his close friends in primary school was Tom Pryde who still remembers one of Oswald's early escapades:

My parents had scratched together enough to buy me a second-hand bicycle, of which I was so proud. After much pleading, I was allowed to take it to school, where I was the envy of most of the other boys, some of whom I graciously permitted to ride it round the playground. Ossie asked if he could have a ride around the street block and with some reluctance I agreed, and away he went in a rather disquieting wobble. I awaited his return with perhaps a slight anxiety, which increased with every minute until I was near to tears. After what seemed an interminable time, my friend arrived back on foot with a part of my lovely bike in each hand and tragically announced he had been run over by a horse and dray! Ossie must have wobbled into the dray. The bike was obviously beyond repair, but Ossie comforted me by saying his brother Lex had a bike which he didn't use much and I could have it! Obviously I accepted his generous offer. I reported the situation to my parents, who were not at all happy about the tragedy and Ossie's generous offer. Their feelings were confirmed by a visit from Ossie's parents that evening. Result – a pedestrian again, but fortunately no break with my friend.

Each year Tom and Ossie competed with each other for top marks, but: 'Ossie outshone me in the final year and became dux of the school.' In 1915 they moved up together to the Southland Boys' High School.

At that stage he began to experience something of the same frustration with the local assembly that troubled his parents. The revival prayer meetings in their home, which had come into being so spontaneously, were opposed by most of the assembly leaders, and Alfred was often taken to task for his involvement in wider evangelistic efforts in the area. This treatment of his father raised Oswald's ire. His own spiritual life had grown little after his conversion so he was in a somewhat dangerous situation and could easily have become discouraged and turned aside. At that critical point two of the Bible class leaders managed to win his respect and provided just the help he needed. 'They saved my life,' he declares.

Meanwhile the bond with his father was deepening. One of Alfred's many Christian activities was running a Sunday School each week at Bluff. Sometimes he would stay on and preach at an evening gospel service, and at times Oswald would accompany him. On one such occasion Alfred had just stood up to preach when who should file into the back of the hall but Charles Alexander, song-leader to J Wilbur Chapman, with several other members of the famous evangelistic team of that day. We can imagine Alfred's discomfiture, but it turned into quite a treat for Oswald, because after the service he and Alfred were entertained to cakes and lemonade in Charles Alexander's cabin aboard the ship that was to take the team on to Australia.

After Oswald had started school, the six years between him and Lex became difficult to bridge. Then, when Oswald was twelve, his brother left for overseas, conscripted for war service. After the armistice, Lex remained abroad studying and working for many years. So the brothers were never very close. But with Rita it was different. Temperamentally, spiritually and in every other way they just clicked with one another.

At high school Oswald's lifelong enjoyment of tennis began. The school magazine lists him and another lad as secretaries of the tennis club. A year or two later he and several friends somehow arranged for a couple of courts to be built opposite his home, and they organised their own club. Now in his eighties, he still enjoys an occasional game.

He continued to do well in his studies, always topping his year in at least one subject and he finished the course with prizes in Latin, French and History. At the end of 1917 he passed the Matriculation Examination, but because he was only fifteen he had to wait another year before he could commence university studies.

When he turned away from farming a rare opportunity opened to him. A Mr Frederick G Hall-Jones, recently returned from war service, had bought a legal practice and needed a law clerk. In normal times applicants for such a position would have been in their early to mid twenties. But the times were not normal. It was 1918 and conscription ensured that practically all young men were away at war. So Hall-Jones had to look for a bright lad below conscription age. He chose Oswald, not yet sixteen.

The longed-for armistice was signed shortly after he started work, but, tragically, the relief and joy that came with the end of the war were quickly swallowed up in the horrors of the influenza epidemic that swept the world soon after. It did not by-pass New Zealand. In Invercargill the loss of life was appalling. Most offices in the city were closed as all efforts were concentrated on survival.

Oswald was co-opted to serve on a vigilance committee established by the city authorities. His responsibilities included such matters as organising the crowds of people who flocked to the committee's office for the throat sprays supposed to help prevent infection. He was also involved in organising help for bereaved and needy families. There was light relief one day when his old French master came into the office and Oswald had to give him certain directions. 'Ah, Sanders,' he said, 'the tables are turned.'

But most of the experiences were grim. He helped to carry the bodies of the dead out of homes, lifting them on to the horse-drawn hearse. He worked in the hospital, and saw the wards where rows of delirious men lay in strait jackets, and the creche, full of newly-orphaned babies and children.

Somehow Oswald escaped infection, despite his constant exposure to the danger, and was ready to resume

24

work in the law office when the epidemic finally subsided.

The practice was prospering. Soldiers were coming back from the war and, with the aid of government loans, were buying homes and farms. Big farming properties were being sub-divided to meet the demand. Hall-Jones was uniquely placed to benefit from the vast amount of legal work created by these circumstances. As President of the Returned Soldiers Association he was a popular and trusted figure in the district. An added advantage was that his firm had been appointed solicitors to the State Advances Corporation, the government agency administering the loans.

In those circumstances it was fortunate that Hall-Jones, earlier selected as a candidate for a Rhodes Scholarship, was a man of great integrity as well as a very able lawyer. He rapidly won Oswald's respect and loyalty.

At the beginning of the academic year Oswald, now sixteen and thus eligible for university entrance, enrolled as an extra-mural student in the Law Department of Otago University in Dunedin, and plunged into law: theory at home by night, practice in the office each day. Responsibility immediately descended upon him. He had to handle large sums of money; probate cases and divorce cases were complex; conveyancing work involved exacting research. Hall-Jones did not spare him. And just as well, for a year or two afterwards, Oswald was left in charge of the business when his boss became seriously ill. He had a telephone at his bedside and there were many urgent calls from Oswald seeking instructions and advice.

It seems almost incredible that a teenager should have carried, and carried successfully, such responsibility. But he did, and in the process gained a vast amount of valuable experience. Those heavy responsibilities also served to draw him still closer to his father. It is pleasant to picture them walking to work together each morning and sitting at home with their heads together of an evening, Oswald drawing upon Alfred's accountancy experience for help with the financial aspects of some troublesome case at the office.

It is at this period of his life that we first gain glimpses of the extraordinary level of energy that many people now associate with the name of Oswald Sanders. As a boy and as a young man he was not robust, frequently suffering from bad colds, headaches and sinus trouble, but somehow he was always able to keep going – he was tough. And he had enormous energy. His office was one floor above street level and he developed a routine of bounding down the stairs and leaping straight on to his bicycle, all in one fluid movement. One day, a friend remembers, this routine was interrupted when, only after he had started his leap, did he discover that the bicycle was not there. He promptly bounded across the street to the police station and reported that his bicycle had been stolen. Later in the day, the police informed him that the bicycle had been found. It was in a certain repair shop where he had left it that morning!

By the time he turned nineteen everything seemed to be in his favour. He had an excellent job, he enjoyed his work and he was able to keep abreast of his law studies. Outwardly successful and buoyant, inside he was covering up deep emotional hurts, and he was spiritually hungry. For some years his Christian experience had not been satisfying; he frequently knew the bitter taste of spiritual defeat. Now the longing for a closer walk with God had become acute.

God's response was just ahead.

2

A Missionary is Born

The special touch of God that began the nights of prayer in the Sanders' home round about 1907 was just part of a much wider movement. Over a period of years, groups of Christians scattered across the island knew times of great blessing. Prayer and a zeal for the spread of the gospel flourished, producing a number of outstanding laymen. In 1908 some of those men banded together to commence the Pounawea Keswick Convention. Ever since then Christians have been gathering there over the Christmas/New Year holiday period to worship together and to hear the Keswick message taught.

Pounawea is a seaside resort on the far east coast of the island at the mouth of the Owaka River, not far from Invercargill. Until suitable buildings were put up in 1929, the meetings were held in a large marquee erected in a clearing in the bush. It was said that nobody ever slept through a meeting in those early days. For one thing, there were no backs to the benches. For another, the mosquitoes were large, numerous and voracious. 'They used to sit on their hind legs and bark at you,' is Oswald's description. Nevertheless, large numbers of people remember Pounawea as the place where the glory of God's provision for us in Christ, through the Holy Spirit, burst in upon them and transformed their lives.

Prominent among the leaders of the Convention was Mr John Wilkinson, a widely-respected Dunedin lawyer. He was prominent not just because of the top hat and swallow-tail coat he usually wore, but because of his remarkably effective witness to Christ. When a man or a woman came to his office to make a will, he would carry out the task efficiently and then quietly ask, 'And what provision are you making for yourself in eternity?' Thus confronted, many a client finally knelt by his desk, accepting Jesus Christ as their Saviour and their guarantor for eternity.

One Christmas, when John Wilkinson was travelling to Pounawea, the train stopped at the rail junction of Balclutha. The platform was crowded with holiday travellers and Wilkinson felt constrained to open the carriage window and call out the words of John 3:16. As he closed the window, a fellow-Christian travelling with him protested that that sort of action was not wise. Wilkinson quietly replied, 'I think I know when God is telling me to do something.' Some months later a lady came up to him and asked if he remembered the incident. 'Very well indeed,' he replied. She said: 'I was in great need at the time, and as I stood on the platform those words came to me as a message from God. They led to my conversion.' That was the sort of man John Wilkinson was, and he was typical of the godly, zealous founders of the Pounawea Convention.

Oswald's father usually attended the Convention, but Oswald had always found some convenient reason for staying away. However, by December 1921 his spiritual hunger had become so great that he decided he must accompany him.

On arrival, he was immediately aware of a remarkable 'atmosphere'. An incident that had occurred in Invercargill a year or two previously helps us to understand that awareness. Alfred had been shepherding a young man from a pagan background who had recently been converted. He was reading the Acts of the Apostles and came to Alfred greatly puzzled saying, 'These early Christians had this keen sense of God's powerful presence, but I don't find it among the Christians here.' Alfred took him to Pounawea. Within a matter of hours he came hurrying up to Alfred, grasped his arm and exclaimed, 'They've got it here, Mr Sanders! They've got it here!'

The principal speaker that year was Rev Evan Harries, a godly Presbyterian minister. He had experienced the Welsh Revival of 1905–6, and his preaching had the touch of the Holy Spirit upon it. He spoke about the vital role of the Holy Spirit in applying the work of Christ on the cross to the daily experience of the Christian. Oswald had heard little or nothing about this area of truth. Now he began to see the glorious possibilities of the Christian life. As the days raced by, the sense of the Lord's presence became almost overwhelming.

The climax came at the missionary meeting. Mr Harries spoke on the Song of the Vineyard, Isaiah chapter 5, and then appealed for young people to offer themselves for missionary service. Along with some fifteen or sixteen others, Oswald responded. 'I made a full yielding of my life,' he says. Ask him what Mr Harries said that moved him so deeply and he will shake his head and say, 'I have no recollection. It was the almost overwhelming sense of God. The warmth of the Lord's presence melted my heart. There came a terrific sense of release, of guilt gone. The sense of the Lord's presence in my heart was so acute that I hardly dared to breathe, lest I lose it.'

He will go on to declare, 'The Lord absolutely transformed my life, the Holy Spirit changed my appetite.' That latter phrase refers to his reading habits. Although Alfred has a good library of spiritual books, they had had no appeal to Oswald; he had preferred other books. Even when under pressure from his law studies and his work, he would read voraciously. But now he was looking for different fare. After the Convention he went off as usual to his uncle's farm for his holiday. In the room his aunt had prepared for him there was a whole shelf of novels. To his surprise he discovered that he was not interested in them, but was drawn instead to the one spiritual book in the room. It was F B Meyer's exposition of John's Gospel, *The Light and Life of Men*. He read it through and thrilled to its message. Then he found that he could now read the Bible for an hour at a stretch – and enjoy it! That put the matter beyond any doubt – God had really met with him. 'I went to Pounawea without any expectations, but my life was completely changed. Pounawea was the turning point of my life.' Like Saul on the road to Damascus, he had been confronted by the living Christ and life could never be the same again.

Back in Invercargill, Alfred's library and his knowledge of Christian books now came into their own. Oswald's appetite for reading was not only changed, but greatly sharpened. There was so much he wanted to know about the Bible, about walking with God, about presenting the gospel to others, about everything that concerned the Christian life. Alfred directed him to Dr R A Torrey's books, especially *What the Bible Teaches*, *The Person and Work of the Holy Spirit*, and *How to Work for Christ*. They were just what he needed and he devoured them. It was not long before he had read everything of Torrey's he could lay his hands on. He liked his propositional style of writing, and the fact that Torrey was a lawyer made him a writer of special interest to Oswald. Recalling his mother's attendance at that meeting back in October, 1902, he laughingly remarks, 'I heard Dr Torrey preach a week before I was born! Now he became my patron saint!'

The library was never allowed to become an ivory tower. From the beginning of his new life, serving the Lord and reaching out to others went along side by side with his reading. He accepted the position of Assistant Treasurer of the Pounawea Convention; he began to attend the lively prayer meeting held at 6.30 every morning in the Invercargill Baptist Church; he started speaking in open-air meetings. Then he and a companion became joint secretaries for an evangelistic campaign which a visiting American evangelist, Dr French Earl Oliver, was to conduct. After the campaign was over and the evangelist had moved on, it was decided to have a series of continuation meetings. It seemed natural to put Oswald in charge and to ask him to speak at several of the meetings.

Meanwhile, law, in the practice and in his studies, continued to demand the larger share of his time. No matter how hard or how long the day in the office might have been, there was always work on the university course waiting for him at home. He developed an ability to study to music – music of his own making! It seems hard to believe that a man could really absorb material from a textbook propped up on the music stand of an organ and play hymn tunes at the same time. But he did and it worked. Of course that was not the only method of study he followed and the overall result was certainly effective. Towards the end of each year he sat the examinations and never failed to pass.

But in the final examination it was a close call. Towards the end of 1922 the combination of his study programme, his Christian work and his work in the law office had just about worn him out. He had conscientiously studied the subject, the Law of Evidence, but he had overworked, and as he walked from the Dunedin railway station to the university his mind suddenly went blank. He could recall absolutely nothing about the subject. It seemed hopeless, but he decided to go into the hall and at least look at the paper. When he had glanced through it he said to himself, 'I can't answer that.' Nevertheless he took up his pen and began to write and went on to answer the whole paper, subconsciously! When it was all over he made straight for the nearest post office and sent a telegram to his parents; just one word: *Failed!* But when the results came out he found that he had gained sixty-five marks and the pass mark was only fifty. That meant he had satisfied all the requirements of the Law Professional Course, and early in the New Year a framed certificate appeared on the wall of his office, declaring to all that he was a qualified solicitor of the Supreme Court of New Zealand.

Hall-Jones promptly offered him a third share partnership, without requiring him to put any money into it. What an alluring proposition! It offered an excellent income, the opportunity to go on to gain barrister status, to gain a Law degree and all manner of brilliant possibilities.

He and Hall-Jones had got on very well together and the close association had only increased Oswald's respect for his employer's high professional standards and moral principles. There had been, for instance, the 'undue influence' incident. Someone had pressured a wealthy old man into making a will in his favour. He had come to Hall-Jones saying, 'Now you draw up his will in this way and I will get him to sign it. There will be 500 in it for you.' The conversation was abruptly terminated as Hall-Jones, without saying one word, rose from his chair, walked round his desk and delivered a mighty kick to the man's rear end.

Oswald may well have reasoned that he could work in partnership with such an upright man. But he declined the offer. Of course his employer wanted to know his reason. 'Well,' said Oswald, 'I'm a Christian and you're not.' 'What the hell's that got to do with it?' Hall-Jones demanded. After Oswald had explained, he was still keen to make some arrangement with this young man whom he regarded so highly. 'Look,' he said, 'there is a practice for sale in Omaru. Suppose I finance your purchase of that and we share the profits?' Again Oswald declined, this time explaining that his main reason was that God had called him to be a missionary.

For some Christians, the alluring prospects that lay before Oswald could not have been put aside without a keen struggle. For him, it seems to have been a fairly simple matter. At Pounawea the Holy Spirit had forged in his heart one overmastering desire – he wanted to be a missionary. He was not merely willing; he wanted it!

During Dr Oliver's evangelistic campaign in Invercargill he had heard that one of the two energetic young men who had arranged his campaign was planning to serve as a missionary. So he spoke to Oswald about the Bible Institute of Los Angeles, where he served as a member of the faculty. He kindly offered to help with the heavy expenses that would be involved should Oswald decide to go there. The idea had great appeal and when he heard that Dr Torrey had left Moody and was now Principal of BIOLA that settled it. He wrote off at once for a set of application forms. BIOLA replied that the forms were being sent, but for some strange reason they never did arrive.

Unbeknown to Oswald there was a Bible training college much closer than Los Angeles. Just a year or two previously the New Zealand Bible Training Institute[1] had been commenced in the North Island, in the City of Auckland. During the summer of 1923–24 he met

---

[1] In 1970 the name of the Institute was changed to The Bible College of New Zealand. Subsequent references to it in this book will use either that name, 'the Bible college', or simply, 'the college'.

several students on holiday from the Bible college. What he heard from them encouraged him to apply immediately. Some time previously, poor health had forced Alfred to give up his job and Oswald had been helping with the family finances, making it impossible to save money. So in his application he had stated candidly that he had only sufficient funds for a few months' fees. The Board of the college, confident that in Auckland this young solicitor would have no difficulty earning whatever he might lack, accepted him.

Auckland stands on a sliver of land that holds the Tasman Sea and the Pacific Ocean apart. Along that isthmus, a string of extinct volcanoes, now green conical hills, enhance the extensive seascapes. Auckland has now spread far beyond the isthmus but, even so, nobody lives more than three miles from the sea. This 'salt water city' is not the capital of New Zealand, but with a population greater than any other it may be considered the principal city.

When Oswald arrived there in April 1924 the Bible college was in the suburb of Ponsonby. Apart from the fact that it was bursting at the seams with an ever-increasing number of students, there was nothing impressive about the timber structure that housed the college. It was the Principal who impressed. Everything about Rev Joseph Kemp was impressive: his presence, his vigour, his faith, his vision, his preaching and his passion for evangelism and for missions.

He was born in Hull, England, and was orphaned at nine years of age. Although he had had just eighteen months of primary school education, he graduated with distinction from the Glasgow Bible Institute, later becoming the pastor of the famous Charlotte Street Chapel in Edinburgh. While there, he visited Wales during the revival and was profoundly affected by that outstanding work of the Holy Spirit. From Edinburgh he was called across the Atlantic and served in turn as pastor of two well-known churches in New York, Calvary Baptist and the Metropolitan Tabernacle.

From there he had accepted a call to the pulpit of the Auckland Baptist Tabernacle which was soon filled to capacity Sunday after Sunday. Then he launched his mid-week Bible study, with 600 attending from all churches. Joseph Kemp's vision extended beyond all denominational barriers, and the many who had been hungry for studies of the whole Bible found satisfaction in these weekly meetings, where printed outlines and notes were distributed.

But Joseph Kemp was too big and his vision too broad to be contained within the work of the Baptist Tabernacle alone. In the impeccable timing of God, opportunity for the wider exercise of his powers was ready and waiting. For some years a number of Christian laymen in Auckland had been aware of the need for a college where young men and women could be taught the Scriptures and trained for Christian service. The need became even greater when many Christian men returned from the first world war eager to serve the Lord. War had toughened them; it had also made them tender towards the world's deepest need. What they wanted now was to be fitted for Christian service. The group of laymen prayed more and more earnestly and looked to God for His response.

When Joseph Kemp arrived in Auckland they quickly recognised in him the answer to their prayers. The gifts and qualities so evident in his ministry at the Tabernacle, were just what were required for a Bible college principal. When they learned that in America he had had experience in the type of college they saw to be needed in New Zealand, that settled it. His enthusiasm matched theirs and in a remarkably short time the college was formally constituted. By early 1922 the first group of students was in residence and lectures had commenced.

Oswald soon found his feet in the totally new pattern of life at the college. Obligations to Hall-Jones had meant that he had arrived at the college well after the beginning of term, so he had a good deal of ground to make up. Perhaps that fact helped to nudge him towards an important discovery he made at that time. It came about because of a gap of a quarter of an hour between the last lecture of the morning and the midday meal. The students used that time for relaxed conversation or an informal game of some sort. Oswald fell in with that pattern until one day he thought to himself that those fifteen minutes could be put to better use. So he started reading a book during that time, moving his bookmark on each day. In two or three weeks the book was finished and he started on another and then another. He had discovered the value of time! The lifelong discipline of redeeming time had begun.

Some may question his wisdom in cutting himself off from his fellow students during that brief period of relaxation. What were their reactions to his withdrawal? On the other hand, they all lived and worked together, day and night, at such close quarters, that there was ample opportunity for fellowship and interaction with one another. Oswald had one consuming purpose – to do his utmost to equip himself for God's service, whatever that might be.

Open-air meetings were an important part of the college training and Oswald threw himself into that work with enthusiasm. The pitch was on the waterfront. It was a tough training ground, for the students had to compete with numerous other groups: Communists, atheists, Mormons and so on. If the gospel presentation was dull, the crowd was soon lost to one of the other groups. In that hard school he learned the basic skills of public speaking – how to use the voice, how to establish rapport with the audience, how to present one's facts and how to sustain interest. More than that, he learned how to apply the truths of the gospel to the real needs of men and women.

One Sunday soon after arriving in Auckland he attended the Baptist Tabernacle. For a young man fresh from the small Brethren meetings in the Invercargill Temperance Hall, it was a moving experience. The Tabernacle, seating 1,400 people, was packed. Extra seats filled the aisles, people were even sitting on the pulpit steps. There was a choir of 100 voices. Most impressive of all was Joseph Kemp; his voice, strong and resonant, filled the church. But Oswald heard within himself another voice saying, 'You will preach in that pulpit one day.' He dismissed the idea as fantasy, but could never quite forget it.

The weeks slipped by and became months. Nearer and nearer came the final date for the payment of his college fees. But he just did not have the money, and his friends were not aware of his need. 'I spent a considerable time in "the dungeon", as we called a dark room downstairs where we could get alone to pray. On almost the last day I came up from "the dungeon" to collect my mail, and in a letter from a friend there was a cheque sufficient to meet my indebtedness! I could not have been more awed had it been $1,000.'

> My need was known
> To Thee alone –
> I called upon Thy name;
> No other heard
> Prayer's whispered word
> And yet the answer came.
>
> Thus secretly,
> 'Twixt me and Thee,

TO FIGHT BETTER

Let traffic grow apace,
That even I
May testify
To Thine exceeding grace.

F Houghton

It was October when, without warning, a telegram from home changed everything. Alfred had suffered a severe nervous breakdown; Margaret could not manage; Oswald must return home. Heavy of heart, he packed his bag, walked out of the college and boarded a southbound train. His student days were over.

3
God's School

The situation at home was worse than the telegram had indicated. Alfred's condition was almost desperate and Margaret just could not cope. Rita had married in 1922 and could not give the sort of help that was needed. Oswald found that he could manage his father, but financial responsibility for all three of them fell upon his shoulders, too. A job had to be found.

John Wilkinson had been a close friend of Alfred's for many years, so it was natural for Oswald to seek a place in his Dunedin law firm. That secured, the home in Invercargill was sold and the trio soon moved into a house in Dunedin. For the next twelve months Oswald slept in his father's room every night, caring for him and slowly coaxing him back towards stability.

But it was a cheerless existence. Alfred, of course, could no longer provide the warm companionship that Oswald had always enjoyed. And he missed Rita, whose puckish sense of humour added an element of fun to the dullest routine. Now he had to provide all the companionship, all the optimism, and there was little or no fun. He was lonely. Not only Rita but all his friends were in Invercargill, 130 miles away.

Jesus said that he is a happy man who does not become upset by the way the Lord treats him. Oswald was not a happy man. For some three months from the time of receiving the 'come home' telegram, he nursed a secret resentment against God. It was not fair. To prepare himself for God's service he had passed up excellent prospects. Now, after only six months in college, God had brought it all to an end. The old pattern seemed to be repeating itself – refusal, frustration – even in his wholehearted desire to prepare himself for God's service.

The 'spell' that lay upon him, spoiling fellowship with God, making his Christian life an empty facade, was broken by a remarkable incident. One night a week the shops stayed open; crowds of people thronged the streets, some to shop, some simply to enjoy the excitement of the noise and bustle. The biggest crowd was always in the 'Octagon', Dunedin's equivalent of a city square. On one such night Oswald was making his way through the Octagon when he came upon a rather pathetic open-air meeting. As he watched, one speaker after another stepped forward and gave a stereotyped, lack-lustre gospel talk. All were absolutely ignored. Then one of them, sensing that Oswald was a Christian, asked him if he would like to 'have a word'. Moved by the indifference of the crowd, touched afresh by the truth of the gospel, he stepped out and began to speak. Immediately he gained the attention of those nearest to him; their interest arrested others. He held their interest and the crowd kept on growing. Soon traffic came to a standstill and the police had to be called in to clear the way. But as Oswald preached the marvellous message of the gospel, and looked out on that attentive crowd, the love of Christ and the grace of God welled up in his heart, pushing aside foolish resentment and restoring fellowship. It was a night never to be forgotten.

Working in Wilkinson's law firm was quite different from working for Hall-Jones. It was a bigger practice, employing a number of solicitors. With Hall-Jones, he had carried large responsibilities and enjoyed considerable freedom. Here he had routine tasks under a senior's direction. 'I had to learn to be a cog in a machine,' he says. Most irksome of all, he soon found that Wilkinson had the true lawyer's regard for detail, whereas Oswald had always been impatient of detail; he preferred to hope that someone else would care for the details. In John Wilkinson's office, he had to be responsible for the details in all matters assigned to him. God had not terminated his student days after all. He had simply transferred him from Joseph Kemp's training to John Wilkinson's. 'I never enjoyed working there, but it was a very useful experience because it gave me the sort of training I needed.'

It was in that law firm, too, that Oswald's long association with the China Inland Mission (now the Overseas Missionary Fellowship) began. Earlier, when the founder, Dr James Hudson Taylor, was still the General Director of the Mission, Alfred had served as honorary Prayer Secretary for New Zealand. So the letters CIM had long been familiar to Oswald. As Chairman of the Mission's New Zealand Council, Wilkinson now assigned this young solicitor of his to work one day a week on CIM business, generously undertaking the cost himself.

The work was largely secretarial, dealing with local matters such as correspondence with donors and missionary candidates, and with arranging meetings for furlough missionaries. Sprinkled through the letters that came to his desk were strange, hard-to-pronounce names of Chinese cities and Chinese pastors. Making sure that he spelt the names correctly in his replies, served to impress them upon his mind. By such an oblique path he gradually came to a basic knowledge of China, and with the knowledge came spiritual concern. John Wilkinson

did not fail to notice that concern and in the following
year invited him to join the Council, and later in the year
Oswald was entrusted with the task of arranging a public
meeting for the visit of the General Director, Mr D E
Hoste. Clearly, God was keeping alive his concern for
missions.

And meanwhile he continued his involvement with
street meetings where he frequently saw the power of the
gospel at work in areas of human need and suffering
far beyond his own youthful experience. But they
strengthened his convictions as to the need for evangelism, and his skills in this area were being steadily honed
to a yet keener edge. Then one day a friend, Frank
Martin, came into his office to tell him that he was
thinking of starting a Christian magazine. Would
Oswald join him in the venture and write articles from
time to time? Before long the magazine, *Maranatha*, was
launched. Both men were young and inexperienced so
perhaps it is surprising that it lasted for three or four
years before expiring. But for Oswald, *Maranatha* had
far-reaching consequences. For one thing, it started him
on his long career as a Christian writer. By the time
Maranatha folded he was no longer inexperienced. Towards the end of the magazine's life it carried an article
by him titled 'The Secret of Continuing'. Looking over it
today, one can imagine many a reader commenting,
'This J O Sanders always has something worth saying
and he says it clearly and concisely.' But the immediate
consequence of the magazine was that it brought him
back into contact with the Bible college. Although his
time there had been so brief, he had maintained a keen
interest in the college, appreciating the strategic importance of its role. It had a prominent place in his prayers.
Typically, practical action flowed out of those prayers.
He encouraged a number of young Christians to apply to
the college and he persuaded a number of other people to

give to the work of the college. All that was before *Maranatha* was mooted. But once it was well launched and the circulation growing, Oswald saw the possibility of using the magazine to make the college more widely known.

In September 1925 he wrote to the college suggesting that an advertisement be placed in a new magazine called *Maranatha*. Payment, he suggested, could be authorised from a small sum he was holding on their behalf. Authorisation was prompt and his letter sparked off something bigger than an advertisement. The college was still new and not widely known; it needed to be promoted. Joseph Kemp and the Board did not take long to see the possibilities in this young solicitor. He was an ex-student, he was spiritual, articulate, energetic and quite obviously concerned for the college.

Within a week he had another letter from Auckland. It offered him a position as Field Representative with the whole nation as his territory. His father's condition dictated Oswald's response, but his letter to Mr Kemp ended with a courteous sentence to the effect that he hoped that one day something like that might be possible. Kemp seized upon that sentence and wrote immediately saying, 'I accept your answer for the present, but I am still convinced that you will one day be associated with us on the staff.' Such a statement from such a man could not be lightly dismissed. Oswald began to wonder – and to pray.

Never a man to surrender a conviction, Kemp soon wrote again, this time in terms so pressing that Oswald had to weigh up the matter afresh and with even greater care. He decided to set apart every evening for two weeks to pray and think about the matter. There were two main problems: Alfred's need of him, and the fact that the new job involved direct solicitation from Christians of funds to build a new college block. Brought up on the Muller/

Hudson Taylor tradition of asking God alone for funds needed for Christian work, he shyed away from that aspect. Then, during that fortnight, he read a biography of D L Moody and discovered that, after fire had destroyed YMCA buildings in Chicago, Moody had gone straight to Christian friends and obtained enough money to rebuild 'before the ashes were cold'. So that seemed to answer one question.

There remained the matter of his responsibility to care for Alfred. How could that problem be resolved? At the end of the two weeks of prayer the conviction had deepened that God was calling him to leave his legal work and join the college staff. It was hard even to think of leaving his father, but the guidance was so clear that he could only conclude that God already had a satisfactory provision for Alfred. Nevertheless it required sheer faith for Oswald to pack his bags and set off for Auckland before that provision was made clear. His father meant a great deal to him, and he was still young in the life of faith, but by mid-February he was on the road. Although the fifteen months in Dunedin had been hard, exhausting, lonely and oftentimes dark, they had developed character and built spiritual muscle.

He decided to start his work as Field Representative of the Bible college by making his way slowly north to Auckland, calling as he went on a number of people whose names had been supplied by the College. After some three weeks he came to the City of Wellington, New Zealand's capital. One night, as he knelt to pray before going to bed, he became deeply impressed with a need to pray for his father, followed by such an atmosphere of spiritual oppression that prayer was exceptionally hard. He sensed the opposition of Satan, and summoned up all that he knew of what the Bible teaches about prayer. He affirmed his faith in the efficacy of the blood of Christ to defeat the evil designs of Satan. He was cold. There was no heating in the room, and he was wearing nothing but his pyjamas, but so intense was the struggle that he could not move; he could only call continually upon God. Finally, after some two hours had passed, the weight upon his spirit lifted and there came the conviction that the battle had been won. Cold and stiff, he was able at last to climb into bed, and refreshing sleep soon followed.

Such had been the reality of the experience that he was not surprised when a few days later a letter came from Margaret telling him that on that very night, the depression that had pressed down on Alfred for so long had been wonderfully lifted. It was not gradual but instantaneous, and it never returned.

Clearly, God had vindicated Oswald's step of faith in leaving his father, and now he was able to move forward with increased confidence. But that encounter with the forces of spiritual darkness was so awesome that it was some years before he could speak of it to anyone.

It was a time of economic recession in New Zealand, and money was tight; not a likely time for an unknown young man to be soliciting funds for a fledgling Bible college. Added to that, Oswald himself was less than enthusiastic. The encouraging precedent of D L Moody notwithstanding, he still found the assignment rather distasteful. But in obedience to the answer God had given to the two weeks of prayer for direction, he stuck at it.

Perhaps his very diffidence and his low-key approach were more effective than a self-assured attitude would have been. Certainly he was effective. Although there were some disappointments, worthwhile gifts to the college were secured. More importantly, friendships were formed that lasted through many years and brought long-term benefits to the college. The name of Oswald Sanders began to be known and trusted.

In one particular city, anxious to keep expenses to a

minimum, he took a room in a distinctly inferior hotel. When he called on the first person on his list of contacts, the man concluded their talk by asking where Oswald was staying. On hearing the name of the hotel he said, 'You can't possibly stay there!' got out his car, drove him to the hotel, had him pack his bags and then took him to stay in his own home. That was the beginning of a warm friendship that continued right through that man's lifetime.

After just six weeks as Field Representative, Oswald received a telegram instructing him to proceed at once to the college. On arrival he learned that Joseph Kemp was about to leave for a visit to Britain and that the position of Secretary/Treasurer had fallen vacant. He was invited to accept that position on a temporary basis. He gladly accepted and threw himself into the work with enthusiasm.

It was an exciting period. The premises at Ponsonby were hopelessly overcrowded and applicants had to be turned away, but more and more promising young people were applying. Expansion was imperative. Members of the Board were diligently searching for a suitable site for a new building, and there were many gatherings for prayer, earnestly asking God for His guidance and for His provision. So there was great praise and thanksgiving when an excellent plot of land in the very centre of the city was secured.

What with consultations on plans for the new building, letting tenders, supervising the construction and raising funds to pay for it all, together with the regular duties of his position, the temporary Secretary/Treasurer was kept at full stretch. His appointment was extended for six months and then 'temporary' became 'permanent'.

From the beginning, Kemp had insisted that the building was to be opened free of debt. If all the needed money had not come in when the building was finished 'then the doors will remain shut until it does come in'. But it did come in and the doors opened on 20 August, 1927. The accommodation for sixty students was immediately taken up.

Once he was settled into a permanent position at the college, Oswald again shouldered responsibility for his parents. Alfred was sixty-five, and although wonderfully restored to a fair measure of health he could not work again. So Oswald bought a house, Alfred and Margaret moved up to Auckland, and soon the trio were living together again.

Much to his delight, Rita and her husband, George Ford, also moved to Auckland at that time. Ever since the early years in Invercargill, George had been Oswald's closest friend so it is not hard to imagine what it meant to him to have their company and their happy home close at hand, with the added pleasure of being uncle to their two little girls, Beryl and Peggy. Their son, Gerald, was born some three years later.

Oswald quickly involved himself in the practical work of the college students. If the best evidence of someone's belief in the gospel is their earnestness in sharing it with others, then the people of Auckland should have been convinced. For a considerable period, each lunch hour the students conducted a meeting on an open area near the centre of the city. Every Friday night the entire student body marched through the streets singing hymns, drawing a good crowd to yet another open-air meeting. Every Sunday morning some of the students gathered street children into a number of outdoor Sunday Schools, sitting with them on the edge of the gutters, teaching them the stories and the truths of Scripture.

In all these ventures Oswald was with the students, encouraging, guiding and helping. That involvement did not go unnoticed by Joseph Kemp and it was not long before he had the Secretary/Treasurer at work in the lecture room, his subject: Personal Evangelism and Evangelistic Preaching.

Nothing better illustrates Oswald's zeal for the gospel than the way in which he spent his college holidays. Starting sometime in 1928, he began to use some of those weeks for evangelistic campaigns in various centres throughout the country. When the last of the students had departed and his secretarial and bookkeeping work was up to date, he would become J O Sanders, Evangelist, and set off to speak at several evangelistic campaigns. God's blessing was upon those ventures and many people came to know Christ and entered into His salvation. That, of course, resulted in requests for more campaigns. Some of the remarkable experiences of those days are recorded in his book, *This I Remember*.

Somewhere round about that time he became aware of a difference in his preaching, a touch from God that drew a greater response from listeners. It had nothing to do with the content of his messages, nor with the way the material was arranged and presented; it was something within the man himself. It was, he says, as though he was now able to project himself into his preaching, just as some singers can so project themselves into the words they sing that they reach the hearts of those who listen. Yet it had in it nothing of self. It came unsought, a sovereign gift from God.

It was at this time, too, that Oswald began to have closer personal contact with Joseph Kemp. Soon after arriving in Auckland, Kemp had launched a Christian magazine he called *The Reaper*. Gradually it became more and more identified with the college until just before his death he made it over to the college. In 1929 Oswald was drawn into the editorial work, and as Kemp was the editor it was work that increased Oswald's exposure to that electric personality. Kemp was a true choleric – forceful, strong-willed, energetic, undeterred by difficulties. His goals were clear and he drove himself, and others, to achieve them. Inevitably, those character-istics meant that he was not easy to work with and Oswald admits that he 'got mad with him' at times. But there was a great warmth about Joseph Kemp and it was just not possible to hold hard feelings against him for long. He found it hard to apologise. But the day after he had said or done something hurtful he would appear with a gift or make some other kindly gesture; that was his apology. And as time went on the two men became very fond of each other.

Perhaps Kemp discerned in Oswald the man to suc-ceed him as College Principal. Certain it is that he went out of his way to train and harden him for rigorous service. Oswald says, 'He was tough on me. He saw that I was soft and spongy. He saw that I needed more iron and proceeded to give it to me!' After Kemp died his widow revealed that some nights, when he appeared to be worried and she asked what the trouble was, he would say, 'I wonder if I have been too tough on him?'

Staff changes in 1929 meant that more administrative work devolved upon Oswald, who was also called upon to take a larger teaching role. He began to lecture in Theology, a series covering the major doctrines of the Bible. It demanded a great deal of study on his part, and the only time available was the last hours of the night. Often he would fall asleep in his chair after midnight, wake up at two or three o'clock and stumble off to bed. Having had only six months of formal biblical studies, his desk now became his theological seminary, the library his teachers, and the Holy Spirit his personal tutor.

It was a hard programme to maintain all through the school year, but he recognised that such intense, ordered

study of the Scriptures was just what he needed. And
seeing students responding eagerly to biblical truth more
than repaid him for his toil. So by the time December
came he was actually looking forward to another year of
the same pattern.

But he was lonely. Much as he enjoyed visiting George
and Rita, their happy family life was a painful reminder
of his own singleness. He longed for the companionship,
the love of a partner. After all, he was now twenty-eight.

4
God's Time

At the Pounawea Convention in 1922, the year after what he calls 'the cataclysmic change' in his life, Oswald had seen and instantly fallen in love with a dark-haired girl named Edith Dobson. Edith was shy and reserved, but there was a twinkle in her blue eyes, hinting at an interesting personality sparkling just behind her reserved manner. Quite unconscious of his watchful interest, she remained efficiently absorbed in her duties connected with the running of the young people's camp. Here was a girl, he concluded, both charming and practical. Sometimes they chatted together among the crowd, but it was all very casual and Edith returned home quite unaware of his interest, much less of his love.

A year or two went past. His love for Edith had not waned, but his determination to devote himself to God's highest purposes had become the dominant force in his life. Because of that he had drawn up what he called his Five-pronged Pledge:

1. I will make no approach to any girl until I know that she is God's choice for me.
2. I will not approach that girl until I know that it is God's time.
3. I will not approach her until I am settled in my own spiritual life, so that it will not bowl me over.

4. I will not make any approach until I know where God wants me to spend my life.
5. I am prepared to stay single, if that should be God's will for me.

Looking back from the vantage point of age and experience, he wonders how wise had been that stand. But for the young Oswald Sanders, determined at all costs to find God's highest purpose for his life, it had seemed to be the only way.

Still more years went by. Usually they were both at Pounawea at Christmas, but what contact they had remained superficial. However, the love that was born from not much more than watching her had grown even stronger. It was an experience well expressed centuries earlier by Thomas Ford,

> There is a lady sweet and kind,
> Was never face so pleased my mind;
> I did but see her passing by,
> And yet I love her till I die.

From time to time he wrote letters to her, but tore them up. 'God held me to my pledge. I just could not get away from it.' It was not only time that tested his commitment to his pledge. Once he was a speaker at a convention in Christchurch. As he sat on the platform, he was suddenly arrested by the sight of Edith entering the church accompanied by a young man! They sat down side by side. Immediately he seemed to hear the devil whispering, 'it pays to wait God's time, doesn't it? Look what's happened.' The meeting seemed to go on for ever. When it did end and Oswald was able to make some casual enquiry, he found that there was absolutely nothing between the two. 'I breathed again!' he says.

The wait for God's time seemed interminable. But again and again impatience was quelled and he came

back to rest upon the assurance that if Edith was indeed
God's choice then He would surely keep her for him.

Early in January 1931 he was on a camping holiday,
accompanying a friend engaged on a surveying job in the
country. It was midsummer. One day out on a hillside he
sat in the shade of a tree reading the Psalms. When he
came to the second verse of Psalm 21 a sudden thrill of
assurance swept through him. 'You have granted him
the desire of his heart and have not withheld the request
of his lips.' In some strange way beyond explanation he
just knew that this was God telling him that Edith was
His choice and that this was His time. He had waited six
years. Now it was time to act. He scrambled down the
hill to his tent and wrote to her.

Edith lived with her parents at their apple orchard in
Omihi, a country district some forty-five miles north of
Christchurch, the principal city of the South Island. Her
high school years were spent in Dunedin, boarding with
friends of the family and returning home for the holidays.
It was a commercial course she followed at school and
her proficiency in typing and stenography opened the
door for a secretarial position with a business firm in the
city. Then a run of bad seasons brought the Dobsons into
difficulties and Edith had to give up her job and return
home to help her parents.

For a girl who had been near the top of her class each
year and who had known the excitement and diverse
interests of the city, life in the country threatened to be
deadly dull. The nearest neighbour was half a mile away;
there was not one congenial young person in the whole
district; there was no church. On top of all that, adversity continued to plague the Dobsons. They barely managed to keep going and there was very little money for
anything but essentials.

Wonderfully, Edith did not just endure those dreary
circumstances, she positively enjoyed life. For one thing,

she had an acute sensitivity to the wonders and the beauties of nature. The endless cavalcade of the seasons brought constant change to the long avenues of apple trees. Stark, bare branches erupted with snowy clouds of blossom which gave way to masses of glossy, green leaves. Then the boughs bowed down with great clusters of green and red apples. Soon the green leaves turned to russet before flying away to signal a fresh start of the whole fascinating cycle. The vast Canterbury Plain beyond the orchard was simply a broader canvas for nature's beautiful, constantly-changing painting. To Edith it was all a never-ending delight.

All the year round she slept on an open verandah and found 'a kinship with the stars'. In the black velvet of the night the stars of that southern sky burned with companionable nearness. Many a night she would lie entranced as

> Silently one by one, in the infinite meadows of heaven
> Blossomed the lovely stars.

But the real secret of her enjoyment of life was an intimate fellowship with God. Her mother was a woman of exceptionally simple faith. Edith learned from her to accept without question the facts and the promises of Scripture and then to depend upon them. The Pounawea Convention of Christmas 1922 – the year after Oswald's crisis experience – had brought a profound deepening of her relationship with the Lord. From that time on, Edith often seemed to be chuckling to herself over some secret joy within. She made no secret of her secret which was, of course, the abiding presence of Christ. Indeed, she was always eager to share it with others. But her apprehension of that great truth seemed to go far beyond the experience of most Christians.

Back on the farm, she joined with her father in serving

the Lord throughout the surrounding district. They commenced a Sunday School which over the years touched virtually every child in the area. They were foremost in inviting preachers to speak in the local hall, and entertained them in their home. There were not many books in the home and Edith was happy to concentrate on the Bible. Reading and meditating, reading and meditating, she acquired an exceptional knowledge of the Scriptures, and in later years Oswald said that he never needed a concordance when Edith was present. She also served as Honorary Secretary of the Missionary Brithday Band, which flourished in those days. This was a system of reminding missionary supporters on their birthdays of a previous commitment to give to missionary work, and it involved Edith in the writing of some 600 letters in the course of a year, including one which began, very properly, 'Dear Mr Sanders'!

Oswald's letter to her came as a total surprise, like lightning out of a blue sky, and just as unsettling. By that time Edith had concluded that God's plan for her was that she should remain single. Clearly her parents needed her help on the farm and it was typical of her that she had accepted that role ungrudgingly as being God's will for her life. She was now happily settled into the role, so it is not difficult to imagine the turmoil that erupted in her heart as she read his letter. But she replied, and other letters followed. At first she regarded them as intrusions into the even tenor of her quiet days. They seemed to threaten the security of the ordered pattern of her life. However, she agreed to his visiting her in May. Three days' leave from the college was all he could manage. Without telling a soul where he was going, he travelled down to Christchurch and there boarded the bus for Omihi. That evening, out among the trees, he proposed to Edith. There was no answer for him that night, Edith insisting on time to think it out alone with God. But the next morning she told him what he had longed to hear: she was to be his and he was to be hers.

That day was far too short for all they wanted to say to one another. All too soon Oswald had to tear himself away, but not before fixing the date of the wedding. Typically decisive, he declared, 'We'll be married before Christmas.' 'We can't,' Edith protested. 'I can't leave my parents. They can't manage without me and they don't have money to employ anybody in my place.' 'We'll be married before Christmas,' repeated Oswald. And then he was gone.

It was back to romance by mail. But at least it was free of the restraints that had inhibited their earlier letters. Now they knew the delight of exploring the depths of each other's heart and mind. How marvellous to discover that despite their widely different circumstances, Edith in her quiet orchard, Oswald in busy public life, there was a remarkable similarity of viewpoints on almost everything. 'We had practically no adjustments to make. In exactly opposite circumstances the Lord had led us along similar lines. We just fitted each other.' There was a deep sense that God had wonderfully vindicated the stand each had taken over the years. Sometimes Oswald's letter arrived at the farm at a very busy time or when her parents were present. Then it would be slipped into the pocket of her apron until she could escape to her room, each tantalising delay made bearable only by gently patting the pocket.

As the year wore on, Edith's excitement grew with every fresh sign of a good harvest. Everything – frost, rain, sunshine – all came at just the right time and in just the right amounts. By December a bumper crop seemed all but certain and, because it was a circumstance limited to that immediate area, market prices would be high. Edith could go off to her wedding with a light heart.

They were married by Joseph Kemp in the Auckland Baptist Tabernacle on 19 December, 1931. Not for Edith the convention of a slow procession down the aisle. There was eagerness in her step as she walked to join Oswald at the front of the church. Teased about it afterwards, she replied with characteristic honesty, 'I wanted to get there! I wanted to marry him!' The strength of her love now matched his. It needed to be strong, for his total dedication to God's will made such heavy demands upon his time and energy that only a marriage built upon true love could have endured its rigours. It did endure and it deepened and was something beautiful to see.

However, it was not a case of a woman accepting, simply for love of her husband, his need to give first priority to God's will. Edith's commitment to the Lord was not one whit less than his. In fact, there were to be times when it was Edith who would hold him to the highest.

She did not have to wait long to discover something of what it was going to mean to share life with this man. Their honeymoon was restricted to just a few days for, with doubtful wisdom, he had accepted an invitation to speak at a Keswick Convention over Christmas week and had agreed that they would go on from there to serve as houseparents at a Scripture Union Beach Mission for something over a week!

Then it was back to Auckland where necessity required that they share their home with his parents. To have to experience the joys and adjustments of their early married life with the older couple always near at hand was hard for them both, but especially for Edith. Knowing there was nothing Oswald could do about it, she simply set herself to rely on God's grace to get her through.

But she had her own problems in keeping up with

Oswald's whirlwind activities. It was 'like being tied to the tail of a comet', she told more than one friend. The shy country girl who had lived so long in her quiet, well-ordered corner was finding she had to surrender the security of well-planned days to the inexorable demands of the pace of life in a much wider sphere. It never became easy. Years later when a friend casually suggested that she must have found her love of order of great value in her busy life, 'No!' was the almost fierce and totally unexpected response. 'With me it can be almost a sin!' She was in fact over-meticulous, a perfectionist living in a world where perfection was rarely attainable. In her own way, she was nevertheless as disciplined as Oswald, and at whatever cost she strove ungrudgingly to keep pace with him.

Now that she could observe the pattern of his life, Edith must have been concerned about the workload Oswald was carrying. In fact they were fortunate that through most of the first year of their marriage his load remained much the same. Heavier responsibilities were just ahead, however, for towards the end of the year there were signs that Joseph Kemp was failing. After the turn of the year he was found to be suffering from a tumour on the brain and in February he lapsed into a coma. The end came early in September. He was sixty-two. He had been such a powerful, dynamic figure, such an effective voice for the gospel, that thousands of people experienced a profound sense of loss. But no one missed him more than Oswald.

During the seven or eight years Oswald had worked under him, Kemp had etched a deep impression on virtually every facet of his life. For whether as preacher, Bible teacher, College Principal or Missions advocate, he was quite outstanding. But much as Oswald admired him and learned from him, he did not model himself upon Kemp. In fact he had decided on his example before he ever met Kemp – he wanted to be like Dr R A Torrey.

It began in the days following the Pounawea 'cataclysm' when *What the Bible Teaches* and other books by Torrey thrilled and built up his heart and mind. Searching for reasons why he found those writings particularly helpful, he discovered that Torrey seemed to have two special abilities. First, he could penetrate to the heart of a biblical passage and secure a clear grasp of the truths it contained. Secondly, he had such a facility with words that he could then make those truths crystal clear to others. Clarity was the Torrey distinctive and it was in that sense that he wanted to be like him. It is a desire that has persisted all through his life. In all his preaching, teaching and writing, every other consideration has been subjugated to his primary concern for clarity.

5

A Leader Emerges

Following the death of Joseph Kemp, Oswald Sanders was appointed Principal[1] of the Bible college. For the second time in his life he found himself thrust into a position of responsibility for which he was ill-prepared. The first time, in the law firm in Invercargill, much hard work, a dash of youthful naviety, telephone contact with Hall-Jones in his sick room, and the knowledge that it was only a temporary crisis, saw him through. This time it was different. How could he possibly carry over responsibility for the college, assume Kemp's classroom work and edit *The Reaper*, as well as continue what he was already doing? It was enough to daunt anybody. It was made worse for Oswald by the deep-seated sense of inadequacy and feelings of inferiority which have dogged him ever since the traumas of his boyhood. Behind his confident appearance he is frequently nagged by a feeling of being basically ill-prepared for the tasks God had assigned him.

Late in life he told how he had learned to cope with

---

[1] Officially he still carried the title of Superintendent. In the interests of interdenominational relations, a Presbyterian evangelist and member of the Board, Mr W J Mains, carried the title of Honorary Principal. But as far as the students were concerned, and in every practical regard, Oswald Sanders acted as Principal, and in 1983 the college honored him with the title of Principal Emeritus.

this problem. 'A sense of inadequacy can be devastating:
It can be a crippling liability or it can be an asset. I've
always had a sense of inadequacy and a certain inferiority complex, on both accounts justified! But it has caused
me to look to the Lord to compensate for the inadequacy.
It has not turned me back on myself, it has turned me to
the Lord. It all depends on your attitude to it. I've found
that when the Lord has asked me to do some new thing
for which I've not had the qualifications; when in conscious inadequacy I've turned to the Lord and said,
"Well, Lord, You're calling me to do it and I'm looking
to You to provide," then, in every case He's seen me
through. That's one of the lessons of inadequacy. It's not
something that the Lord takes away. He doesn't neces-
sarily make you feel adequate, but He does see you
through.'

He had no doubt that God was calling him to this new
task, so looking to God to see him through, he threw
himself into it. He may have lacked 'paper' qualifications, but he had certain other invaluable qualities. The
most important was a heart for the work. Earlier he had
been puzzled that despite every effort on his part, his call
to missionary service had never been realised. More
recently he had come to see that the task of training other
young people for such service was the way in which God
was going to fulfil His call. So he was enthusiastic.

There were other qualities, too. He had a good mind,
well-developed study methods and a retentive memory.
His legal training had taught him how to analyse a
problem, isolate the principal elements, and reach valid
conclusions. Not least, he had a remarkable capacity for
hard work, his seemingly endless stores of energy often
astonishing those close to him.

Now it seemed as though the hand of God drew all
those elements together, and enriching them all with His
grace, made the inadequate adequate.

His added classroom responsibilities tipped yet more weight into his already heavy study programme. Needing to teach Greek to slow learners, he began to add to the little Greek he already knew, often keeping just one jump ahead of the students and occasionally being caught out! With the Homiletics course he sometimes followed a ploy Joseph Kemp had used. Two hapless students would be sent out of the room for a minute or two while a topic was chosen. They would then be called back and told to give an extempore address on the subject. One day when two students were thus despatched, one said to the other, 'I have an idea that Mr Sanders will say that he is a dying man and that I must tell him what he must do in order to be converted.' Sure enough, when they were called back Oswald began to declare solemnly, 'I am a dying man . . .' At which the man blurted out, 'I thought so' – and brought the house down.

All this time he kept up a steady programme of reading, in addition to his heavy routine of lecture preparation. Most of the great evangelical authors were read and their riches carefully indexed in a comprehensive filing system he evolved for himself.

How in the world did he fit all that into his busy schedule? The answer to that question is also the key to understanding how he has coped with the even heavier schedules of subsequent years. It all goes back to that discovery in his student days at the college of how much could be done in the fifteen minutes of free time before lunch each day. That practice of 'redeeming' time was steadily developed. He studied everything he could find on the subject, experimented and finally evolved a pattern suited to his circumstances and then set out to live according to that pattern. No financier ever gave more careful thought to the most profitable ways of investing his funds than Oswald gave to the investment of his time.

The new Principal must have appeared a rather formidable figure. Tall, erect, brisk and purposeful in his movements, he was always neatly dressed, his high forehead topped with tight, dark curls. But it was the piercing eyes behind the narrow-rimmed glasses which held the students. One of the men from those days says: 'No matter where one sat in the lecture room, it seemed that his eyes were upon you and if by any chance you had something troubling your conscience, you felt quite certain that he knew all about it.'

That disconcerting notion was no doubt reinforced by the sternness of his manner. A couple of years earlier Oswald may have thought that Kemp saw him to be 'soft and spongy' (probably a highly fanciful thought on Oswald's part), but it is quite certain that no student ever had such an impression. Photographs of the period and student recollections all suggest a rather forbidding, no-nonsense appearance.

After all, it was a training college. Students came there not just to be taught but to be trained. Missionary service was seen to require men and women able to live and work in hard, exacting conditions without losing their glow, their cutting edge or their Christian grace. So most students expected the training to be fairly rigorous. It had been so under Kemp and they quickly saw that it would be so under Sanders.

Nevertheless, he was only thirty-one and some of the students were older than that; and he did have a distinctly youthful appearance. So it may be that he allowed himself to appear somewhat more formidable than he really was. There were few hints, for instance, of the strong humorous streak hidden away behind that stern exterior.

Long before joining the staff he had been widely known as 'Ossie'. When Kemp first called upon him to give some lectures he had warned, 'Now you mustn't allow the students to call you "Ossie".' 'If I have to make them call me "Mr Sanders" in order to control them,' he replied, 'then I'd better not take the job.' Kemp need not have worried, for Oswald had no difficulty in controlling them and no student ever dared call him anything but 'Mr Sanders'. Among themselves they usually referred to him as 'J O'.

When he became Principal he introduced what he called 'The Clinic'. Each Wednesday morning he gave a talk which was deliberately subjective. He spoke about some of the problems of the Christian life, such as pride, or despondency, or greed, exposing the students to the searching, probing light of Scripture. He set out to help them see themselves, to recognise faults, failures and areas of weakness. Having thus diagnosed he would then put before them God's remedies and urge their application.

Sometimes he varied the approach by summarising the life story of an outstanding Christian leader. But the purpose was the same. He would trace in those lives the 'surgery' or the 'medication' that had resulted in spiritual health and vigour.

It was quickly apparent that Oswald had a remarkable gift for such work. He could apply with telling effect the truths of the Bible to the practical matters of life. So the probes touched many a raw spot, many a hidden, sensitive area and, of course, caused pain. But it was hurt that led to healing, if accepted as coming from God. In fact many students look back on those Clinic sessions as the best, the most helpful hours of their college days. 'I used to crawl back to my room, get down on my knees and pray about what I had just heard,' one student remembers. But Oswald did cut close to the bone and there were a few who bitterly resented it, some even going so far as to say that his stern disciplines placed a barrier between himself and the students. Nevertheless there were many who accepted the disciplines and built upon them lives of outstanding service.

Complementing and balancing the Clinic was another weekly session, the worship hour, at 8 o'clock on Sunday mornings. The talks he gave then were just as deliberately objective as the others were subjective. Here the emphasis was always on looking away from oneself to the great facts of God: who He is, what He has done and what He has promised. The intention was to warm the heart, quicken devotion and prompt worship.

They were memorable times. Oswald recalls one particular Sunday when his own devotional period at home had been especially rich. Arriving at the college, he stood up and announced the hymn 'O Come All Ye Faithful', intending to use those few minutes to compose his thoughts. But the words of the hymn and the message he was about to give touched his heart with peculiar force until he was quite overwhelmed. The tears began to course down his cheeks. Not a man who weeps easily, on that one occasion he just could not stop. As so often happens in life, this specially solemn moment had a comical twist – he discovered to his distress that he did not have a handkerchief! One of the students obliged, and the hour that followed was an unforgettable time of heartfelt adoration and worship.

Again and again there emerges, particularly in this earlier period of his life, an enigmatic mixture of warmth and coldness, sensitivity and censoriousness. During the repressive years of his boyhood Oswald had spun a tight cocoon around himself; the warm, easy, laughing personality emerging only in the 'safe' company of close friends. To others he appeared somewhat stiff and reserved. Little wonder that students hesitated to approach him. It was to take almost a lifetime to shed that cocoon, but from the time of his engagement to Edith it began to loosen. A lady who knew them both says, 'They were very, very much in love. It developed him and he became a much more normal kind of man. Although Edith was shy, she really brought him out.' That was a continuing process, of course, and it was now helped forward by the magical touch of a baby.

John Wilbur, their only child, was born on 21 September, 1936, and the students soon became aware of a subtle change in their Principal. The staff, too, began to detect signs that the baby was softening, mellowing their Chief. On the day of Wilbur's birth the men, greatly emboldened, seized Oswald, dressed him up in makeshift 'baby clothes' and trundled him around the campus in a wheelbarrow. Appreciating the spontaneous warmth of feeling behind the prank, he joined in the fun and a few days later proudly carried Wilbur into the common room for the students to admire.

The picture of a stern, reserved person must not be overdrawn, for those sombre colours were relieved by soft, warm tonings. For one thing, there has always been a great kindliness about the man. One couple still remember vividly a college picnic, the one day in the year when men and women students were free to talk to one another! The couple were all but engaged and he was soon to sail for China, hoping that she would be able to join him later. So they had much to say to each other and were making the most of the rare opportunity when Oswald walked by. Without a word, he took the fellow's arm, placed it around the girl's shoulders, and walked on.

Another student remembers the night he came before the council of the China Inland Mission as a candidate for membership. That has never been a relaxing experience, but in those days cross-examination by a roomful of conscientious council members was a specially daunting prospect. But it was Oswald who came to call the nervous student for the interview and walking back with him to the council room he laid a reassuring arm on his shoulders and whispered, 'You have nothing to fear.'

A very young lady, called unexpectedly to face the same council, was overcome with nervousness, and a question about an obscure passage in Revelation left her speechless. Oswald, the youngest of the men around the table, gently intervened: 'Perhaps, Mr Chairman, after Miss—— has graduated she may be able to answer that question!' And while it was true that they were scared of him, many a student in real need was surprised by the warmth of his sympathy and understanding.

But it was his consistent example that made the deepest impression. They could all see that he was disciplined, diligent and prayerful. They knew that he was walking closely with God and that he was seeking to win men to Christ. 'He was not only our teacher,' one of the men recalls. 'He was our model, our pattern.'

Many who were his students sum up the way they felt about him in pretty much the same words: 'I feared him, but I loved him' – perhaps the supreme accolade for a Bible college principal.

All the editorial work on the college monthly was now Oswald's responsibility. Like all magazines, *The Reaper* was both insatiable and tyrannical, ever demanding more copy and always relentless about deadlines. Some articles could be drawn from other sources, but Oswald had to provide a considerable share. So he just had to write and God used that necessity to lever him into the role of author, a role that was to have a wider significance than he could possibly have imagined.

When he first became Editor, he was lecturing in personal evangelism so he rewrote his notes and published them as a series in the magazine. Readers responded enthusiastically and urged him to produce the material in book form. The result was his first book, *The Divine Art of Soul Winning*, which appeared in 1937. It was very well received, first in New Zealand, then overseas, and has run into many editions, including German, Afrikaans, Hindi and Hungarian versions.

In the meantime, the board room was fitted out with shelving so that it could double as a bookroom, making Christian books available to the public for sale. Here Alfred came into his own, sharing his extensive and intimate knowledge of books, and charming staff and customers alike with his sunny, gracious manner.

Complementing the Christmas period Pounawea Convention in the South Island, is the Ngaruwahia Easter Convention in the North. Some eighty miles south of Auckland, Ngaruwahia is a beautiful area at the junction of the Waipo and Waikato Rivers. From its inception in 1921 there have been very close links with the college. In fact through the year the administrative and clerical work of the Convention was for many years handled in the college offices, and staff members played a vital part in the platform ministry.

It was at Ngaruwahia in 1931 that Oswald's world-wide ministry as a convention speaker began. The following year he was appointed Chairman and the convention became a high priority in his life. He usually wrote the group Bible study materials; he conducted the missionary meeting and the testimony meeting and, of course, was frequently one of the speakers. At Ngaruwahia he rose to great heights, his gift for bringing scriptural truth to bear on the practical issues of life helping many Christians to a vital turning point in their experience.

Oswald was concerned about the low level of missionary support and he became interested in the possibility of introducing to the 1935 Convention a faith promise scheme. The idea was to encourage Christians to ask God to show them individually how much extra they should undertake to give regularly through the following year. They should then trust God to make it possible for them to give that amount.

Typically, Oswald concluded that he could not exhort others to do something he himself was not doing. So three months before Easter he explained the idea to Edith and asked her, as the one who managed the family house-keeping, to nominate the extra amount they should covenant to give each week. At the time they were working on a very tight budget, just barely managing to scrape along, but he had decided in his own mind that they should commit themselves to an extra five shillings a week. After thought and prayer, however, Edith came back to him with the conviction that the amount should be ten shillings a week. He was quite taken aback, wondering how they could possibly give that much. But to Edith he simply said, 'If you think we can do it, that's fine.' So, without telling a soul, they started on that basis.

At the end of the first month they received out of the blue a cheque for the extra they had given, exact to the penny. At the end of the second month, and again at the end of the third month, they received back in one way or another all they had given.

So when Easter came he had no hesitation in urging others to a similar step of faith. The scheme became a regular feature of the Convention and resulted in many wonderful stories of God's response to faith and in a considerable increase in funds for missionary work.

Evangelism still took a large slice of his time. He was constantly preaching the gospel, constantly seeking to win men and women to Christ. Apart from the missions he conducted in the college vacations, and as well as the student open-air meetings, he was closely associated with the Eady Hall Mission. This was an interdenominational effort that grew out of a mission conducted by

Rev W P Nicholson a year or two earlier. A vital evangelistic meeting was held each Sunday night in the Lewis
Eady Concert Hall on one of the main city thorough-
fares. In 1936 a larger venue, the Roxy Theatre, was
engaged. But the missioner, already well past retiring
age, could no longer continue. Oswald was appointed to
take his place.

He tackled the task with enthusiasm, rising to the
challenge of fitting in to his already crowded programme
the preparation of a major evangelistic address every
week. It also involved arranging the student participation, organising the teams of volunteers who walked the
streets inviting passers-by into the theatre, and supervising the counselling and follow-up of those who
responded to the gospel. It was thrilling work and
he loved it, but it drained off considerable time and
energy.

Edith watched with alarm. Surely there must be a
limit to the load one man can carry? She was right and
her fears were well founded, for without realising it he
had shouldered more than he could carry.

Just at that critical point a severe blow fell. George
Ford, Rita's husband and Oswald's closest friend since
boyhood, contracted spinal meningitis and died within
three days. Rita was left with three children aged thir-
teen, eleven and seven. Her only assets were the household furniture and the one week's wages George had
brought home on the night he fell ill. There were no
savings: during the grim Depression years they had
surrendered his life insurance policy to get them
through.

Now the brother and sister relationship that had been
so close from early childhood became closer than ever.
Rita found, as many others have subsequently found,
that he is a great man to have with you in a crisis. He was
a tower of strength, comforting and encouraging her

with the great truths of God's unfailing love and care, and helping with all the practical issues of her difficult situation.

They lived on opposite sides of the same street at that time and the Ford children still remember how 'Uncle' used to call in every morning on his way to the college. 'He used to race in the back door and out the front.' In fact the children now 'discovered' their uncle. Up till then he had been largely taken for granted, respected because of their parents' obvious respect, but not really known. Now he made time to be with them. They remember riding with him in the old Buick that belonged to the college and coaxing him into switching off the engine about half a mile from their home to see if it would roll down the hill, round the corner and just mount the rise to the house. He was fun to be with and they were somewhat puzzled that the college students seemed to stand in awe of this man whom they knew as always ready for a lark.

It was only when he had Rita and the children settled that the shock of his own loss burst in upon him. George Ford, his most intimate friend, was dead. Oswald was devastated. Immediately, the years of intense effort, the crowded schedules and the unrelieved burden of innumerable responsibilities all began to take their forfeit. He began to lose weight and went on to drop fifty-six pounds. Some nights Edith wept when she saw him stripped.

Still he failed to read the warning signs and set off on a nationwide lecture tour he had arranged for the long college break. In His mercy, God intervened and sent one of His servants to save him from his folly. Dr John Laird had been the leader of the Scripture Union Beach Mission where Oswald and Edith had been house-parents just after their marriage. A warm friendship begun there had steadily deepened over the years. Now 'by chance' they suddenly came face to face in Christchurch. Dr Laird saw at a glance that he was ill and over-strained so he asked, 'What are you doing?'

'I am on a lecture tour,' Oswald replied.

'You are *not*.'

'I *am*.'

'You will cancel every one of those meetings.'

'I can't. I have arranged them. Some I can cut out, but there are some I can't.'

'You will cut them all out. If you don't, I will. You are on the brink of a nervous breakdown.'

That shook him. He agreed to cancel the tour and listened carefully as the doctor went on to say, 'There is only one thing that will recuperate nervous exhaustion and that is rest and sleep. You can take any medication you like, but it won't do you any good. You must have rest and sleep.'

Oswald and Edith went to the Dobson farm at Omihi. At first he couldn't even digest milk and water, but slowly Dr Laird's prescription took effect and at the beginning of the new term he was able to resume his responsibilities, but only with difficulty. The long, hard climb back to full strength was to take nearly two years.

The college Board also recognised the need for drastic measures and minuted a decision '. . . that Mr Sanders be prohibited from doing any work of any kind between Friday night and Monday morning'. He has no recollection of that edict, which probably means that he did not abide by it, but he was chastened and with some difficulty disciplined himself to a more moderate programme.

What really helped was the Board's decision to promote Mr Leslie Rushbrook to the position of Secretary/Treasurer. Back in 1935 Oswald had asked the Lord to guide him in choosing from the graduating class a man to work under him as administrative assistant. He was

drawn to Mr Rushbrook because of his spiritual qualities, his good mind and his ability to get things done,
and the Board asked him to start as Assistant Secretary
in the New Year. Within weeks Oswald was in no doubt
that God had answered his prayer for guidance. Rushbrook thrived on hard work and, nothing loath, Oswald
off-loaded many time-consuming tasks. Now his promo-
tion, after two years' experience in the office, made it
possible for Oswald to delegate more of the heavier
responsibilities. Edith was delighted.

6

A Man Who is Growing

Towards the end of his two-year recuperative period he was back to bounding up stairs two or three steps at a time. And just as well for he was committed to speak at two conventions in Australia over the 1939–40 Christmas/New Year holiday period.

He and Edith went first to the Upwey Convention in the Dandenong Ranges near Melbourne. Although it was his first visit to Australia he was not unknown. By that time his second book, *Christ Indwelling and Enthroned*, was in the bookshops and that, together with his widely-read earlier volume, ensured that many people were keen to hear this man.

They were not disappointed. Both the man and his message made a deep impression. One of those present at the convention was Mr Leonard Buck, a Melbourne businessman and leading Christian layman, who later became closely associated with Oswald in a number of Christian ventures. Then a young man of about Oswald's age, Leonard Buck had already made his own mark upon the Christian life of Melbourne and was known throughout Australia for his wholehearted commitment in the field of Christian service.

'When I first heard Oswald at Upwey,' he recalls, 'I thought: here's a vital young man who means business with God; he's God's man. You knew that God was talking to him and that he was listening – and obeying. You knew that he was trusting God and that there was a sacrificial element about his faith that was quite distinctive. It did not matter what the cost; obeying what God said was all that mattered.'

The climax of the convention was Missionary Day and Oswald was asked to give the closing address. He had been amazed to learn that the missionary offering at the previous convention, attended by some 1,400 people, had amounted to only £300. So he concluded that his address should tackle this matter of giving to missions.

After referring to the financial needs of missionaries, and the sacrifices they had to make, he went on to urge that their sacrifices should be matched by sacrificial gifts from other Christians. 'If missionaries are called upon to make sacrifices, should we be called upon to sacrifice nothing? How much did you sacrifice for missions last year? What did you do without?' That led on naturally to the introduction of a faith promise plan. He had many telling illustrations of the way such a plan had been successfully followed over recent years at Ngaruwahia and he quoted encouraging testimonies of how God had wonderfully provided for those who participated in the plan.

The offering followed. Great was the excitement and great the thanksgiving when it was announced that the cash and pledges amounted to £1,600, more than five times the figure of the previous year. The Convention Chairman, Dr J J Kitchen, often said of Oswald in the years that followed, 'He taught us how to give.'

The impact at the Katoomba Convention in the Blue Mountains west of Sydney was equally impressive. Although the attendance was much less than at Upwey, the missionary offering was more; £2,300.

Such remarkable events were, of course, reported in

the religious press and the name of J Oswald Sanders began to be etched on the minds of a widening circle of Australian Christians.

At home he was now the recognised head of the Sanders-Dobson-Ford extended family and all manner of family responsibilities devolved upon him. In 1940 Edith's parents decided they could no longer work the orchard and would have to retire. But all Mr Dobson's efforts to sell the property had failed. Would Oswald please help? He hurried down to Omihi and within two days had put a proposition to one of the Dobsons' neighbours and concluded a satisfactory sale. He then arranged for a house for the Dobsons to be built beside his own home in Auckland.

Shortly before that, Sandy had arrived back in New Zealand. He had lived abroad ever since going off to serve in the first world war. Now, with his English wife, Doris, and their small son, Ian, he was hoping to make a new start in life. They had no resources, so Oswald and Edith took them into their home and shared what they had until Oswald helped him find a position in Wellington.

The happy sequel to the story is that after some years in Wellington Sandy was wonderfully converted. For decades his name had remained high up on the prayer lists of Alfred, Margaret, Rita and Oswald. Now they were filled with gladness and thankfulness. Sandy went on to demonstrate the reality of his conversion by living out the rest of his life in earnest devotion to Christ, serving Him in every way he possibly could.

The next family crisis was not a happy one. Alfred, grown very deaf, was struck by a tram as he was crossing a road in Auckland. He lived on for a year-and-a-half until his death in 1944, but he was unable to move and barely able to communicate. The blithe, buoyant spirit, no longer able to sing, to talk or to read was severely tested. Gerald Ford remembers his uncle sitting beside Alfred prompting him with endless patience through the great verse, 'All things are?'

'Yours.'

'And ye are?'

'Christ's.'

'And Christ is?'

'God's.'

That intimate picture shows a very different side to the brisk, capable and rather cool person he sometimes appeared to be.

But he could be tough. When George Ford died Oswald saw that it was essential that Beryl, the eldest child, should leave school and get a job. The family said he was harsh and resisted the idea. He insisted. And, of course, he was right. In coming years that capacity to take hard decisions and ride out the ensuing storm was to be tested in issues of much wider consequence.

Round about that time he and Edith were grappling with an exceptionally difficult problem in their home. Someone with whom they were obliged to be in close daily contact was making life almost intolerable for them. Crisis after crisis would build up and engulf them in exhausting scenes. It came to the point where they felt that if allowed to continue it might well destroy them and the work God had called them to do. Yet despite every effort it did continue. Finally they concluded that this was an attack of the adversary. It was a situation, they agreed, which was not glorifying to God, and which called for the exercise of the Christian's authority in prayer; for taking a stand against the enemy; for holding on to God and claiming the victory of the cross over the enemy.

So at the beginning of each day, together they adopted that position in prayer. Then they saw God's restraining hand come into action. Sometimes they would see the familiar signs of another crisis building up and then to their astonishment it would suddenly subside. The problem was not removed, but it was restrained. 'It taught us a lesson in prayer that perhaps we could not have learned in any other way.'

At the outbreak of the war in 1939, he was beyond the age for conscription and although he offered to serve as an Air Force chaplain he failed the physical examination. Doubtful his health may have been, but there was no question about his energy. His third book, *The Holy Spirit of Promise*, came off the press and helped many readers. He was appointed Director of The United Maori Mission; he was Chairman of the New Zealand Council of the China Inland Mission; on convention platforms and in church pulpits he was a channel of blessing to a great number of Christians, and throughout the land he was effective as an evangelist.

Behind this expanding ministry, however, was not just abounding energy, but personal growth. His walk with God, his biblical insights, and his spiritual discernment were all deepening. Side by side with that growth came continuing development of his gifts and capacities.

All this, he maintained, was due to three factors: the godly influence of a number of close friends, the intercession of certain people who had undertaken to pray regularly for him, but, above all, the sovereign blessing of God.

That was true. But it was also true that part of God's blessing was the ability to discipline himself, for that was both spur and bridle to all the other gifts and powers God had bestowed. The iron discipline he had clamped on himself after his conversion was rarely relaxed.

Mr Rushbrook recalls that as a student he had recognised that the Principal was a well-disciplined man. But it was only when he began to work with him in the office and saw him close up in a range of stressful situations that he came to realise the strength of the grip he kept upon himself.

There was a warm, friendly relationship between the two men, so that Rushbrook felt all the more keenly the chill wind of censure that blew briefly after an incident in the office. He had recently developed a more than friendly interest in another staff member – the young lady who later became his wife. And one day when, as he felt, she was treated unfairly by an older woman, he over-reacted and spoke much too hotly in her defence. Afterwards, Oswald's anger cut deeply when he inveighed against Rushbrook as the disturber of peace in the office. Then, seeing his misery, the stern mask cracked and he laughingly added, 'But after all it was vicarious, wasn't it, Les?' It was a rare glimpse of the real Oswald Sanders; happy-natured, fun-loving, struggling against childhood repressions, and coping with responsibilities beyond his years, by self-imposed disciplines he seldom relaxed.

Part of that discipline was a determination to correct anything in his life that would detract from his usefulness to God. An amusing instance of this is still remembered by his niece, Mrs Peggy Ford. When quite young, she was taken one day to one of Oswald's meetings. Instead of paying attention to what 'the great man' was saying she became fascinated by his mannerism of constantly buttoning and unbuttoning his suit coat. She kept a careful tally and afterwards told him the score! He never did it again.

But he was no stuffy super-saint. It was a college custom that the lecturing staff were served morning and afternoon tea in what was referred to as 'the inner sanctum' – the Matron's sitting room. Miss Annie Grantham was a rather formidable lady and it was some months after Les Rushbrook joined the staff before she considered it proper for him to be admitted into 'the inner sanctum'. When that privilege was finally conferred he watched goggle-eyed as Oswald and Mr Henry Yolland, the Dean of Studies, wrestled furiously until, panting and laughing, they crashed to the floor and the Principal triumphantly seated himself on the Dean's chest. Les Rushbrook was no less astonished to notice that the staid Matron seemed to enjoy to the full these remarkable goings-on. It was, he discovered, a not unusual occurrence; a wholesome safety valve for them all.

The Upwey Convention Council was keen for Oswald to return for the 1940–41 Convention, but wartime restrictions on civilian travel across the Tasman ruled that out. Then in 1943 air travel made it possible for Oswald and Edith to accept a renewed invitation and they received an enthusiastic welcome when they arrived at Upwey just before Christmas. Despite the shortages and difficulties brought about by the years of war, attendance was excellent and Oswald and Edith were greatly encouraged by the warm response at every one of his meetings. Again on this occasion he gave the main address on Missionary Day and the offering reached a new record of £4,360. Even more encouraging was the large number of young people who offered themselves.

But for Oswald it was his meeting with Rev John Deane which remained the most memorable feature of that Convention. They were teamed together as the main speakers and during the ten days of meetings they really got to know one another. Mr Deane's background was very different from Oswald's. He had been a high school Classics Master before entering the Baptist ministry in the state of New South Wales. Now he was Vice Principal of the Baptist Theological College of that state and was also minister of one of Sydney's better-known Baptist churches. He had academic degrees in both Arts and Divinity.

But just as each man's convention addresses complemented the other's, so the two men experienced a remarkable meeting of minds and blending of spirits, and Oswald returned to Auckland holding John Deane in high regard.

He was soon into the collar again and the year began to race by. Then letters from Shanghai brought news of a proposed visit to New Zealand early in 1945 by the General Director of the China Inland Mission, Bishop Frank Houghton. W J Embery, Home Director of the Mission for Australia and New Zealand, was to accompany the Bishop. Oswald immediately set about drawing up an itinerary for the two men, including opportunities to address the Ngaruwahia Easter Convention.

It is significant that a recent incident had confirmed him in his respect for the CIM. As Chairman of the New Zealand Council he had felt, initially, that a young couple who were ex-students of his had been unfairly dealt with. But when he received a copy of the minutes of the China Council, he discovered that leaders who had come from all over China to discuss important affairs affecting the whole Mission, had spent almost an entire morning in prayer and deliberation about this couple. Such a mission surely merited his support. And now he was to meet its present General Director.

Bishop Houghton proved to be a warm, friendly man, scholarly, well-informed and possessed of that quiet charm which accompanies true godliness. Oswald took to him at once. They travelled together around New Zealand for some weeks until one day the Bishop dropped a bombshell – would Oswald accept appointment to the position of Home Director when Mr Embery retired in the coming year? While that came as a total surprise to Oswald and Edith, it was no sudden impulse on the Bishop's part.

In December 1944 the Mission had suffered a severe blow when three of its workers, including Graham and Elsie Hutcheonson of Melbourne, Australia, were killed in a plane crash in China. Graham Hutcheonson had had the spiritual gifts and the wide experience that would have made him an obvious choice for a future Home Director, but that was not to be, and Mission leaders were continuing the search for God's man. While in Australia, the Bishop had heard glowing reports of Oswald's convention ministry, especially his strong missionary emphasis. He had seen him in action at Ngaruwahia and watched him at work in the college. He could not but notice that wherever he went Oswald was esteemed and appreciated. He no doubt heard, too, that in 1941 Oswald had been spoken of as one of the two men whose work for God in New Zealand was most influential at that time. The other was Oswald's close friend and advisor, Dr John Laird. And as Bishop Houghton later told Oswald: 'When I am considering inviting a man to take on a position like this, one of the first things I ask is: Is he growing? I could see that you were growing.'

Bishop Houghton and Mr Embery then departed, leaving Oswald and Edith to wrestle with the question of what their response should be. What did God want them to do? As they prayed and opened themselves to God's direction they both discovered, somewhat to their surprise, that growing within them was the conviction that they should accept the appointment. But it would have to be a decision based entirely on faith, for every outward consideration was against it. They were happy and fulfilled in their work, they had no desire to leave Auckland and live in Melbourne and, as they soon discovered, all of their family and friends, without one exception, were convinced it would be wrong. 'Why,' they said, 'you would be leaving a larger job for a smaller.'

It was one occasion when guidance had to be totally

independent of circumstances and of the counsel of others, and entirely dependent on their inner perception of God's will. Without any outward factors to encourage, the inner conviction persisted until they felt compelled to accept.

For Oswald especially, it was a highly emotional issue. After all, the work of the college was not just a job, it was his life. He had grown with the college; the college had grown with him. No wonder he broke down while announcing his decision at the board meeting. All through the years he had enjoyed a very happy relationship with the board. A number of the members were close personal friends. So his announcement was deeply felt. Then one of the men suggested that it would be out of character for God to enrich the CIM by impoverishing the Bible college. Surely, he said, if this decision of Oswald's was God's will then He would have someone suitable to take his place. Did Oswald have any such person in mind? At that moment an idea which had been forming in his mind crystallised into a conviction and he was able to reply, 'Yes, I do. His name is John Deane, Vice Principal of the Baptist Theological College in Sydney. He is admirably suited to this position.'

Subsequent correspondence with Mr Deane was to reveal that in a truly remarkable way God had been preparing him for just such an invitation. He was, in fact, ready and willing to accept.

Other encouragements began to appear. First, the reactions of relatives and friends began to change. The Dobsons assured Edith they would be able to manage by themselves and Rita invited Margaret, her mother, to live with her.

Then they were greatly heartened by an incident which is best told in Oswald's own words.

The previous year I had purchased for the college a three-storeyed building on which a sum was still outstanding. I said to my wife, 'Wouldn't it be wonderful if someone would give the balance owing on that building, so that I would be able to leave with all the college property free of debt?'

Two or three days later I had a call from a friend of the college asking how much was still owing on the building. When I told him the amount, my delight can be imagined when he said, 'My sister telephoned me today and said, "Wouldn't it be good if Mr Sanders could leave the college with the debt on the new building paid off. You find out how much is owing and I will give you a cheque."'

All in all, it seemed as though God had waited until that step of faith had been taken before confirming that their perception of His will was correct.

There was one other very important element in this momentous change in their lives. It seems to have only come to the surface, or perhaps only assumed its full significance, after their decision was taken. That element was his Pounawea call to missionary service. Through no fault of his, that call had never been realised. The first few sentences of his address on Missionary Day at Upwey in 1939 reveal something of the depth of his feelings.

I entered the New Zealand Bible Institute intending to go to South America as a missionary, but the Lord did not accept the offering of my life for that purpose, and sent me back to business. It was a great disappointment to me at first, and I was grieved at the Lord's dealings. But I thank God today that although I am not a missionary, yet I can do something to help missionaries. I have three passions; one is to preach the gospel, another is the passion for helping Christians into the fulness of life that there is for them in Christ, and the third passion is to help forward by every means in my power the missionary enterprise.

It seems as though he had concluded that the call was to be realised at some level other than direct participation. And it is clear that he was no longer in dispute about it with the Lord of the harvest. But wistful thoughts and longings persisted somewhere well beneath the surface.

Two of the college graduates remember the day when they were setting out for missionary service in China. '"J O" was among the crowd seeing us off. As the ship drew away from the wharf we saw him standing alone, behind the crowd. We were touched by the rather sad expression on his face. He wasn't sad because we were going but because he was staying. He longed to go as a missionary himself, but year after year he had to watch others go forward.'

Now, twenty-five years after Pounawea, God had opened the way to a much closer involvement in missionary service. The call would still be something less than fully realised, but it was a giant step towards it.

And the college? With real humility Oswald maintained that John Dean would bring gifts of scholarship and discipline beyond anything he himself could offer. The change, he insisted, could bring only good. Nevertheless, Oswald had already consolidated the work begun by Joseph Kemp and had built well upon the foundations.

It was also true that there would always be a part of himself that was bound up with the life of the college. It was hard to leave.

7

The Horizon Widens

It was March 1946. All over the world, in every town and city, men and women were returning from the armed forces to civilian life and a daunting shortage of housing for their young families. Oswald was well aware of the problem that could face his own family. On arriving in Sydney, Australia, en route to Melbourne, there was still no word of where they were to live. As usual, they brought their need to God in prayer and then nine-year-old Wilbur confidently suggested, 'Perhaps God already has a place for us, but He's keeping it a secret!' 'Perhaps He has,' agreed Oswald, mentally adding that he certainly hoped so. It was difficult not to be anxious.

On arrival at Spencer Street Station in Melbourne, they were told that a Christian businessman travelling overseas had made his beautiful home available to the Sanders family. Wilbur was jubilant. 'So God *did* have His secret place!' he crowed, while a grateful Oswald acknowledged to himself that there had been a world of difference between the child's prayer of faith and his own weak prayer of hope. It was a lesson he never forgot. They now had a clear six months during which to take stock and make plans.

The next few months tested Oswald's patience to the full. The job was indeed smaller and less demanding than the one he had held for so long, but even so he had to learn the inside workings of the CIM and meet its constituency throughout the states of Australia. One thing he learned was the unexpected size of Australia, roughly 2,500 miles from east to west and about as far from north to south. Not even Mr Embery's unfailing graciousness could lessen the frustrations of the tedious round of meetings, as they travelled the long distances from city to city by public transport.

'But it did me the world of good,' says Oswald. 'For too long I'd been too much my own boss. By force of circumstances, all the way through, I had to take the helm in our own home when I was quite young. I was the peace-maker. Then when I went into business, I was thrust immediately into responsibility. Indeed all the way through I had been thrust into responsibility without any preparation for it.'

Now he was facing the responsibility of directing the home side of a missionary society without having had any field experience, not even a visit. He could handle young candidates, but how would seasoned veterans, some his senior by years, react to his leadership?

It was only natural that there were some murmurings from a few older missionaries who found his business-like manner rather difficult to accept. Accustomed for years to the slow, indirect approach of the east where time was not considered, it was somewhat disconcerting to find this young man dealing courteously and efficiently with their affairs, and then just as courteously bringing the interview to a close. All that was necessary had been said. There was no small talk. Time was a valuable commodity!

One of these older missionaries was the Rev J W Tomkinson who had for some time been giving much needed help in the Melbourne office. He had been born and bred in China and had worked there for most of his life. He vented his feelings about these new fangled ways in Chinese mutterings, to the secret entertainment of Oswald's private secretary who shared the outer office with Mr Tomkinson. But it was not long before Oswald came to appreciate the prodigious amount of work taken care of by the older man and dignified his labours with the title 'Federal General Secretary'. 'After that I could do anything I liked!' recalls Oswald. Nevertheless his secretary continued to wish she could understand Chinese!

However these low rumblings found no echo at council level. Dr Leon Morris was much in demand to serve on mission councils and found them all a great trial. But the CIM council was different. There were no woolly wanderings down unprofitable by-paths under Oswald's chairmanship. 'His acute mind saw straight to the heart of a problem. "*This* is the point under consideration, *not* that or that," he would say.'

Right then Oswald's energetic leadership swept through the Australian scene like a strong, fresh breeze. Another very busy council member wrote of him: 'Mr Sanders brought to his new office a clear and well-ordered mind, a rich biblical ministry in writing and preaching, a sane and balanced approach to all kinds of spiritual issues, and a wide knowledge of missionaries and prospective candidates.'[1]

The distinctive feature of his ability as a councillor, and especially as Council Chairman, was his complete objectivity. Never did he become emotionally involved in issues that were being debated. His ability to remain analytical and dispassionate served to keep the point at issue clearly in focus. It was an ability which was to be

[1] Sir Marcus L. Loane, MADD, *The China Inland Mission in Australia and New Zealand 1890–1964*.

increasingly valued throughout the whole Mission in the years to come.

It was not surprising then that the job began to grow with the man, and as an inevitable corollary the man grew with the job. Already known as a convention speaker, he began to receive many invitations from churches and Christian organisations, and Oswald saw to it that he was recognised as the Home Director of the CIM. The Christian public's perception of the work of the Mission grew and widened.

Hand in hand with this went his unflagging zeal in preaching the gospel. A man who is today an active OMF council member recalls: 'One aspect of Mr Sanders' ministry was his gospel preaching. For a number of years he was a regular speaker at Youth for Christ rallies, and at one such rally both my younger brother and I committed our lives to Christ through his ministry.' And then he adds a very significant comment: 'Another aspect that I observed was the Christ-likeness of Mr Sanders. I remember him coming to our home and he was a gentleman in every sense of the word. This had a profound effect upon me as a very young Christian.' Indeed it is a delight to meet today a number of mature, active Christians who date their conversion from a time when as teenagers they heard his clear, urgent presentation of the gospel.

He was welcomed by young people wherever he went – to Christian Endeavour Conventions or to IVF[1] Conferences. Dr Paul White, then secretary of IVF, tells of watching Oswald spend a good deal of time talking with informal groups between sessions. A number of those students have for years held significant places in

---

[1] Inter-Varsity Fellowship, now known as Australia Fellowship of Evangelical Students (AFES).

academic and professional spheres. It is of particular interest that one of them, David Stewart, became Principal of the Bible College of New Zealand in 1965, and is by far its longest-serving principal.

And in view of all that has been said of Oswald's forbidding appearance, it is impossible not to add that the handbook of the National Christian Endeavour Convention held in Perth, 1949, carries a photo of Mr J Oswald Sanders – a handsome young man with clear, alert eyes, and a mouth that is ready to smile!

Invitations to speak came from all over Australia and continued to increase even more after his appointment in 1947 as Chairman of the Upwey (later Belgrave Heights) Convention. He served on a number of Christian councils, notably that of the Melbourne Bible Institute.[1] This brought him into close contact with leading Christian businessmen; their keen minds met and melded in their zeal to promote God's work on every front. Successful in their business careers, they had forward-looking vision, impatient of the shackling bonds imposed by rigid adherence to the status quo. If change would advance the cause of Christ without surrendering one iota their loyalty to Him and His word, then change there should be. The effect upon Oswald of the close friendship of such men was invaluable for the man and for the work he grew to love.

Another friend with whom he established a close rapport was Dr Paul White (*Alias Jungle Doctor*). As Christian writers, they had much in common and maintained a lively correspondence. Oswald's secretary at that period recalls one letter from Dr White which began: 'Thieves have broken into the IVF office, the children are down with measles, I have a bad bout of

---

[1] Since re-located and known as The Bible College of Victoria.

asthma and my wife's illness has worsened. But "God is still on the throne"!'

The most important influence upon his life and work came in 1947 when he visited China. Bishop Houghton saw the immense value of such a visit for both Oswald and his British counterpart, Fred Mitchell, who combined running a successful business as a manufacturing chemist with his work as British Home Director. Both men travelled together and found each other's company enjoyable and stimulating. Oswald conceived an immense regard and respect for his older companion and learned a great deal from his wisdom and experience.

Of course, the greatest impact was made by China and her people, as day after day he travelled from one city to another, through towns and villages, through the countryside, and so right up to the north-west, to the borders of Tibet.

Always, everywhere, there were people, people and more people; he seemed to be never out of sight of people. Never before had he understood so clearly the immensity and the urgency of the task to which he had committed himself. To be able to speak at meetings, albeit by interpretation, thrilled his missionary soul. Most moving of all were the conventions of tribal people, now known in China as 'minority groups'. Hundreds, sometimes thousands, of people walked for days over mountain paths to enjoy a few days of fellowship in worship and song, and to hear the word of God expounded. To share in such ministry was an unforgettable privilege.

Even more impressive were the Christian students who held such potential for China's future. In several cities he was both thrilled and humbled by opportunities to speak by interpretation to groups of two or three hundred students. The missionaries, for their part, were astonished at the response of these young people to

Oswald's messages. He was clearly a man who spoke in the power of the Holy Spirit.

There were happy visits with Australians and New Zealanders, some of whom had been his students. And if the latter wondered how he would react to the stark realities of missionary life, they found him adaptable, appreciative, undemanding and ready to listen and learn. In all, it could only be described as a transforming experience; speaking about China could never be, and never was, the same. Before, he could speak convincingly of what he had heard and read; now he could speak with authority and deep heart conviction about what he had seen and heard. It changed his attitude to the training and preparation of candidates; he saw the need for regular candidates' courses, and he found in himself a greater understanding of the personal problems with which missionaries constantly grapple.

The trip did not end there. After China it was on to Britain and North America. But en route there were other stops. He flew from Shanghai to Hong Kong in the depth of a cold winter, wearing all his warmest clothing to save surcharge on his overweight baggage. The next leg of the journey was by sea-plane to Bangkok, then an hour and a half, through boiling heat, in an open truck, to the city hotel. 'I thought I was going to die!' he said. But he didn't, and next day it was on to Singapore to speak at a week's meetings. One night two young Chinese, a brother and sister, were among those who came to the Lord. Their father, Dr Benjamin Chew, a prominent Singapore physician, was present, and he was so stirred that he gave Oswald £250 as a thank offering – enough to cover his travel expenses for the whole trip. More significantly, it was the beginning of a friendship which years later resulted in Dr Chew, at Oswald's invitation, becoming the first Asian council member of OMF.

In England he saw Fred Mitchell against his own background as a widely-read man with an extensive library and a great sense of history. He took Oswald to many notable places, such as John Bunyan's home at Elstow and the Moot House, with its worn wooden lectern and seats around the walls, where Bunyan had held his Bible classes. They visited Mother Wilson's house where John Wesley had preached. And Oswald's childhood memories were stirred when they visited The Old Curiosity Shop; he recalled hearing how his great-grandfather had spent holidays with Charles Dickens. Then they went to Fleet Street and The Old Cock Tavern where the floor was spread with sawdust as in Dickens' day. Fred Mitchell had booked the table around which the great novelist and journalist used to meet with his friends.

Oswald took another smaller step back in time when he visited the London headquarters of the Mission at Newington Green. In 1871 God had provided several adjoining houses in Pyrland Road for the London centre, but as time went on Hudson Taylor became more and more concerned about the lack of any room large enough for a prayer gathering of any size. But though he had to wait for several years, God's answer was to embrace much greater things, and in 1895 a new building had been opened in Newington Green. It had been designed and built to meet the Mission's special needs, and incorporated a prayer hall that seated 160 people. To enter the door of that hall, with the Mission's motto: 'Have Faith in God', boldly emblazoned above the dignified entrance, was like stepping close to the beginnings, the very heart, of the work God had called into being more than eighty years before.

Then there was the visit to the Keswick Convention, where he spoke on his favourite theme of missions. Thirty years later a prominent Bristol surgeon reminded

Oswald of that occasion: 'It was the most expensive sermon I have ever heard!' Through it God had prompted him to double his missionary giving, and he had done so ever since. A very expensive sermon! But perhaps it was the opportunity to observe Fred Mitchell in his role as CIM British Home Director that left the deepest impression, and he summed up the whole visit as 'mind-expanding'.

The trip to Canada and the United States was 'an awakening of both mind and spirit'. He had always liked and got on well with the Americans and Canadians whom he had met, so he enjoyed meeting with men and visiting places that had previously been known only through the pages of North American periodicals.

But there is a limit to what any man can absorb in a series of fresh encounters, one after another, month after month. The trip had been too long; ten months in all. There was only time to catch his breath after arriving home, before plunging into preparations for the 1947–8 Convention, the last to be held at Upwey. Nevertheless, with hindsight a few years on, those ten months were to be seen as immensely valuable, for in that time he had met all the Mission leaders, on the field and at home, as well as most of its members. He had become known as a person, just as he was already known as a writer, with four books published up to that time.

In the following year it was evident that he had indeed absorbed an amazing amount during those ten crammed months. Everywhere people wanted to hear what he had to say and his diary for 1948 was soon filled. Seven new workers had gone from Australia in 1947; eight followed in the next year. Young people responded keenly to Oswald's Bible teaching ministry. Interest in the Mission was at a high level when ten more new workers left Australia for China in 1949.

Combined with his other commitments, Oswald's

programme as CIM Home Director was now quite formidable. But he was not yet working at full stretch, so when he was approached during the following year with a new proposition, he was more than ready for it.

The Keswick Book Depot was an important focal centre for the Christian life of Melbourne; in particular, the Belgrave Heights Convention operated from there. However, as a commercial proposition, the bookstore had been slowly running down. Would Oswald take over the management? His quick, incisive mind saw at once where the problems lay and he knew he could deal with them. He saw the advantage to the Mission of his being self-supporting – it was a time of rapid expansion and funds were low. After praying about it, alone and with Edith, he was ready to approach Bishop Houghton who very soon agreed to this new move.

Oswald immediately brought his business expertise and his experience with the college bookshop to bear on the financial side of the Book Depot, while his confidence and drive gave the needed boost to staff morale; business began to flourish again. A weekly radio programme, together with staff incentives, proved so successful that he began to expand the business, opening four more stores in Victoria and neighbouring states.

In Melbourne, the bookstore was only half a minute away from the CIM office, and he combined visits to the other stores with Mission affairs in the same areas, at business expense. He certainly wasn't only a back-room manager. He was often in one of the stores, chatting warmly to customers, answering questions and introducing them to new books. Like Alfred, he never found it difficult to chat about books! Not that everyone found him easy to approach. His expression was naturally serious in repose, and combined with his tall, broad-shouldered build, this tended to distance him from people. As one friend observes, 'His smile is at its best on recognition,' and it was not easy for people to reach that point. On the contrary, aware of his spiritual stance, it *was* easy, as another friend has neatly expressed it, 'to feel oneself to be an inferior model'! Of course he had long ago learned not to wear his heart on his sleeve, but neither was he the distant, austere figure some imagined. An incident recalled by his friend, Leonard Buck, is very revealing. One evening, during this period when Oswald was Chairman of the Belgrave Heights Convention, the speaker delivered a message straight to the hearts and minds of his listeners. After he had sat down, Leonard Buck, who was leading the meeting, felt impelled to ask any who had sensed God had spoken specifically to their hearts, to come to the front. Oswald quietly rose from his seat on the platform, went down the steps, and took his place with others who had come. 'He was weeping,' recalls Leonard Buck. 'It was the only time I ever saw him weep; the man ran deep.'

Oswald had indeed become a greatly-respected figure as a speaker and writer – a fact his fellow missionaries were quick to appreciate. And they welcomed his leadership – whether it was the harassed Mission Home Hostess running a busy household with little or no assistance or the secretary with a complex problem that needed to be brought to a council meeting that evening. In the first case Oswald quickly sized up the situation and sent the husband out at once to buy a washing machine and a floor-polisher. In the second, he sat down straight away, and in front of the secretary's amazed eyes, quickly wrote a lucid presentation of the whole complicated situation. He was always busy, but always ready to listen to problems relating to field or home, and missionaries facing difficult personal problems found him sympathetic and supportive.

Welcome, too, was the added zest he had infused into the annual public meetings held in each city. These had

long been a high spot in the year for many Christians.
Now, with Oswald's time-conscious approach applied to
them, they gained in smoothness and efficiency, and
woe-betide missionary speakers who went beyond their
time limits! His own closing address, the climax of the
meeting, was equally closely tailored within its time slot.
It meant that people could relax and get the most out of a
meeting that they knew would end on time and allow
them to chat with a friend or two before hurrying off to
make that vital train, tram or bus connection; an important factor in a day when most people still depended on
public transport.

Inspired by the British models, Oswald had established regular candidate courses in Melbourne, as well
as annual weekend prayer conferences in the various
states. These conferences continue to play an important
role in drawing the Mission's prayer supporters – the
very life blood of its work – close to its heart.

The CIM in Australia had never stood higher in
public esteem. But it had already entered the stormy
period of the greatest crisis in the history of foreign
missions in China.

8

Good in a Crisis

The first day of October, 1949, has been written into history as the day when Mao Zedong stood on the parapet above the great square in Beijing and proclaimed the People's Republic of China, the beginning of a completely new era in that land. At first, a number of optimists, including Oswald, hoped that the Mission would be able to continue its work. The policy of the Mission had always been to stand aside from internal politics in a country where they had always acknowledged themselves to be 'guests'. Could they not continue to do so? But the '1948-ers', as the group who had arrived in China that year were known, had never been able to leave the city of Shanghai, while the '1949-ers', who had flown straight into the western city of Chongquing, were still confined to their language school on the outskirts of that city. They were the last CIM recruits to enter China.

As 1950 dawned, other missions were beginning to withdraw personnel, but as late as the Australian August issue of the Mission's paper, *China's Millions*, Oswald wrote: 'Can new workers enter China? For the present the answer is no . . . Workers at present on furlough are also unable to enter . . . While we have so many workers in China and the Lord continues to give such evidences of the Spirit's working as we continue to see, there is no intention of seeking fields elsewhere ... There is no intention of voluntarily quitting China.' But the situation changed so rapidly that by the end of the year it was clear that the continued presence of Western missionaries was a serious embarrassment to the Chinese church and the long, slow process of withdrawal began.

Meanwhile, Bishop Houghton, who after full consultation with all his fellow directors carried the final responsibility for all major decisions, was ill. Persistent insomnia had forced him to leave Shanghai in April of that year, and seek rest and restoration in Australia. He and his wife spent three months with the Sanders, who gave him the quiet and seclusion he needed, in the pleasant home they had built beside the Mission home on the steep, grassy banks of the Yarra River at Hawthorn. Oswald describes his condition as 'a clear case of burn-out', and he was far from recovered when, at the end of the year, he called a conference of Mission Directors to meet in February, 1951. The venue was at Kalorama, in the beautiful Dandenong Ranges just outside Melbourne. It was a barely representative gathering; just five Home Directors, Bishop Houghton and his Deputy China Director, John Sinton. No other field leaders had been able to leave China.

Years before, his sister Rita had said of Oswald, 'He's a great man to have with you in a crisis,' and now the Mission was at crisis point. Not that any of the men at that conference, least of all Oswald, had any idea of the part he was to play in that crisis. Quiet and unassuming, Oswald has never been a scintillating 'personality plus' man. Only as men rub shoulders with him is the solid gold beneath the surface revealed. Then, he was just the 'new boy', the youngest and least experienced of the group. However, he proved himself a very competent minute secretary and equally articulate in discussion.

While acknowledging that for the present at least it was impossible to consider advance in the China field, some conference members were hesitant about looking at other areas for possible advance, lest that should prejudice care and support for the more than 600 members of the Mission still in China. Oswald and others, however, could see that once the Mission family began to move, it was going to be imperative that their leaders should be ready to offer new directions. Using a metaphor from the recent world conflict, he urged upon his fellow-directors the need to keep up the momentum of this active missionary force. 'We are a fighting force,' he maintained, 'and our Commander has the right to withdraw His forces from one area and deploy them in another, and to open a "second front" by means of which to attack from another angle.' Slowly, after days of prayer and discussion, they came to accept the idea in principle. But Japan? What of Japan? Some of the directors still in China felt such a move might not be wise and those at Kalorama were still unsure when they took a mid-morning break during which the mail was handed to Bishop Houghton. After they had re-assembled, the Bishop shared the amazing news that two of the letters contained large gifts ear-marked for advance into Japan's wide-open door, and one specifically stated that half the amount should be used for the initial expenses of a survey of that country's spiritual needs. It was an awesome moment. Their great Commander was indeed on the move, and they must follow. A cabled communique was sent to all Mission centres: 'Lengthen cords, strengthen stakes. While emphasising prayer for China, conference unanimously convinced Mission should explore unmet need preparatory to entering new fields from Thailand to Japan.'

By the beginning of April 1951 some 300 workers had left China, and by the end of the month Bishop

Houghton had gone to Hong Kong where emergency headquarters had been established. Survey teams were implemented and redeployment of forces was beginning.

By the latter part of the year the greater part of the CIM membership had left China and it was obvious that a fully representative conference should be called to ratify and extend the decisions taken at Kalorama. All Home and Field Directors, plus one representative from each home country, were called to meet in Bournemouth, England, during the latter half of November 1951. Oswald, with Walter Michell, whom he had appointed executive general secretary in Australia, joined twenty-three other men for this momentous conference.

From the start all were acutely conscious that the outstanding need was to ensure positive leadership for the unknown path ahead. Bishop Houghton had never fully regained his strength, following his breakdown in the previous year.

It was soon evident that polarisation between field and home representatives could threaten to split the conference down the middle. At first Oswald had frankly regarded the field men as 'a bunch of mavericks', but as discussion continued, he came to appreciate their problems. Although the decision cost him dearly on the personal side, after a few days he openly shifted position. Soon he and Fred Mitchell found themselves thrust willy-nilly into positions of leadership as the field men looked to them to lead the conference out of the impasse while matters of policy were being thrashed out.

They were difficult days when the whole conference agonised over matters that had to be resolved. 'It was really the birth pangs of the new Mission,' is Oswald's summing up. On 29 November they finally accepted Bishop Houghton's resignation from his position as General Director. 'He has been a spiritual leader greatly loved and trusted,' wrote Fred Mitchell in a supplement to the December *Millions*, 'but the conference felt it would be unfair, both to himself and to the Mission, to face the future without the fullest assurance that he was able to carry the very heavy responsibilities involved in his office.'

For the remaining two days of the conference, when a phenomenal amount of work was dealt with, Fred Mitchell was asked to take the chair on the first day, and Oswald on the second. The matter of the appointment of a new General Director was deferred, but it was recognised that total responsibility for the affairs of the Mission was too much for any one man. Henceforth the responsibility for work on the fields was to lie with the Overseas Director. The General Director, when appointed, would have oversight of all other matters. This left Arnold Lea, Overseas Director, as acting Chairman of the Directors, with Rowland Butler as Assistant Overseas Director. The Home Directors would lend assistance as a steering committee.

Thus began the new phase of the Mission. It was essentially the same body in that its principles and practice remained the same, but a name change was obviously necessary as the Mission no longer functioned in China. It was to be known as the Overseas Missionary Fellowship of the China Inland Mission.

When Oswald returned home, eager to promote the work on the new fields, he found that the momentum had certainly not slackened. Some ex-China missionaries who were not needing a break went straight into work among Chinese in the new fields, and 1952 saw seven new recruits from Australia, including four for Japan! Interest in the work and the demands on Oswald's time continued to grow.

Then another conference of all Home and Field Directors was called for May 1953, to meet in the new

International Headquarters in Singapore. Again Oswald enjoyed Fred Mitchell's company when they were given opportunity to visit the new fields.

When the conference met, no new General Director had as yet been appointed; no one name seemed to stand out clearly above others. Arnold Lea, with more than twenty years of field experience, was an obvious choice that would have been welcomed by the whole Fellowship, but he was too valuable in his position as Overseas Director; there was total agreement on that point. Perhaps they should look among the Home Directors? Oswald took fright at that suggestion and hastily declined to be considered. Finally the conference ended with still no decision on the matter.

When the Directors were preparing to leave Singapore, it was suggested to Fred Mitchell that if he changed his booking to a 'Comet' flight – that faster aircraft was still a newcomer – he could breakfast with his wife a day earlier! Oswald was at the airport to see him off, before he himself boarded a plane for Hong Kong, where not many hours later he heard that the 'Comet' had crashed after take-off from Calcutta. There were no survivors.

Oswald felt keenly the loss of his friend. Through him and through other Mission leaders: Arnold Lea, Rowland Butler – the list is too long to enumerate – he had been greatly enriched and enlarged, both mentally and spiritually. Looking back over the seven years as Home Director, he realised that not only had the scope of his work widened, but his own vision and capacity had grown broader and deeper. They were years when he had learned something of the agony of missionary leadership; when almost every major decision involved the lives of people; 'not just *any* people, but people who were your friends'. They were decisions that involved sleepless nights, deep heart-searching and, above all, supreme confidence in a great God whose unfailing faithfulness daily met inadequacy with His own strength.

Meanwhile, six more recruits sailed from Australia that year and more and more young people were offering themselves for service. But before the next party sailed in November 1954, the council of Field Directors meeting in Singapore in April of that year, had unanimously invited Oswald to accept the position of General Director.

Oswald's immediate reaction to the invitation was one of amazed incredulity. These men, all of them gifted and widely experienced, were asking him, 'a little pebble from "down under", with no missionary experience, no missiology course, to undertake such a position of leadership. It seemed quite absurd and a terrific gamble.' He was flooded by a sense of total inadequacy.

But as he settled to thinking the matter over quietly, he admitted that the very fact that men of such calibre had been led by God to such a unanimous position, demanded a careful and prayerful response from him.

Certainly, they had greatly honoured him. He remembered the moment at the 1953 Singapore council, when he had instinctively recoiled from the very thought of such a possibility, and he knew that he was backing away from the cost involved.

Then there were Edith and Wilbur to consider, and the great disruption this would bring to their happy family life. How he longed to be able to sit down and talk and pray over the matter with Edith. But the news had reached him in New Zealand, where he was speaking at a series of meetings, and she was at home. Letters would have to suffice. But they both found it helpful that each had to obtain guidance separately, and as they shared their thoughts in letters, each found the other was being inexorably drawn to the same conclusion – not of choice, but by the Spirit of God. Oswald's old friend, Dr John

Laird, was a fellow-guest in the house where he was staying, so Oswald was able to share the matter with him. Before John Laird left, he told Oswald he believed he had a special message for him from God. It was in 1 Peter 5:1–7, a passage especially addressed to Christian leaders. After he had gone, Oswald went to his room and read the passage in the then recently published Phillips translation. He was brought up sharply when he read in the second verse: 'I urge you then to see that your "flock of God" is properly fed and cared for. *Accept the responsibility of looking after them willingly and not because you feel you can't get out of it.*' He knew it was God's answer to his fears and his nagging sense of inadequacy. He had neither desired nor sought this position. Years before, when a very young man, he had toyed with the idea of applying for an attractive position that seemed to be tailored to his gifts and abilities, and there were friends who would use their influence on his behalf. Then suddenly God had brought him up short. He was walking down Queen Street, Auckland, and he still remembers the very spot where he stopped dead in his tracks: 'Do you seek great things for yourself?' was God's challenge. 'Seek them not.'

From that day on, the words from Jeremiah 45:5 have been one of the lodestars by which he has checked his guidance. 'If God is in it, you don't have to work your own passage,' became one of his maxims. And now, he was sure beyond all doubt that God was in this. In joyful trust he accepted both the privilege and the responsibility, and in the years to come when the going got rough, he could look up and say, 'Well, Lord, you got me into this and I'm counting on you to see me through.'

Edith's faith and courage in accepting the decision fully equalled Oswald's. For her, the years in Australia must have been richly fulfilling. She enjoyed the comfort and privacy of their home on the Yarra banks, and

Wilbur had been free from the constant attention of two sets of grandparents, one living with them, the other alongside. He was enjoying school life at Carey Grammar, and excelled at his studies, eventually setting a school record by winning every exhibition open to him. He had inherited the family musical gift and enjoyed exercising his talents at the piano and in choral music. The home was a place of warmth and fun, with Edith at its centre.

It was in Melbourne, too, that her deep knowledge of the word of God, and her close walk with Him found full expression. She became chaplain of the Kew Baptist Homemakers' Group and spoke regularly at a group made up largely of the wives of leading Christian laymen. Sometimes she gave a lively review of a book she had enjoyed. It all helped to develop her latent gifts as a speaker and she was especially appreciated at the women's meeting at the annual Belgrave Heights Convention. The most outstanding of these addresses was given on a return visit from Singapore.

In the impeccable timing of God, that message, which was on the sovereignty and omnipotence of God, was given at Belgrave Heights *after* the Convention had received the news of an accident in New Zealand in which Rev John Deane, Oswald's successor at the Bible college, had died. Some weeks earlier, when Edith had awakened one night in Singapore, God had given her the whole outline of the message. Based on Acts 12:1–17, it bore the unmistakable marks of the Spirit of God. The circumstances of the time drove home that message to the hearts of all who heard it. John Deane, travelling only a few miles to speak at a convention, had died in a car crash. Her own husband had travelled thousands of miles in safety.

Along with this ministry, she had developed a circle of valued friends. She was happy and secure. And then this bombshell. For the second time in her life she had to face uprooting from a world she knew and loved. But such was her trust in the Saviour with whom she had walked for so long, that at the age of fifty, she confidently put her hand in His and set out on this new and untried way. It was her choice. That was always her way. Once she recognised that any course was in the will of God, nothing could deflect her from it. She was one with Oswald in accepting the invitation.

9
Mission Leader

I. CONSTANTLY ON THE MOVE

They left Melbourne in the last week of August, travelled overland to Perth and sailed from Fremantle for Singapore on 1 September 1954, more than thirty years after Oswald's Pounawea commitment and his subsequent rejection of the Hall-Jones 'golden offer'. Self-doubt still kept him from understanding how his previous training and experience could possibly be adequate for what lay ahead. But among many passages from Scripture and from other reading that had stood out for him during the preceding three months were sentences such as: 'When God has spoken, to hold back is not humility, but unbelief,' and, 'Obedience is the one condition of blessing.'

Edith had read a similar thought written by an old pioneer missionary: 'Nothing so clears the vision as obedience to the revealed will of God.' She had quoted the words when she had spoken at the crowded farewell service in Melbourne's Collins Street Baptist Church. It happened to be her fiftieth birthday, but her quiet voice carried a ring of steel as she went on to say, 'When I said "Yes" to this new and difficult request, a flood of light came into my heart.'

The Australian Christian weekly, *New Life*, wrote in its report on the widely representative gathering: 'By his frequent visits to various states, by his ministry at many conventions and meetings, as well as by his books and writings, Mr Oswald Sanders has made a profound impact on Christian life throughout Australia, and will go forward to his new ministry . . . assured of the earnest prayers of all who have benefited by his ministry in the past eight years.'

That meeting had marked the climax to a time of such activity that Oswald could hardly believe that only three months had passed since his appointment had been ratified. He had had to find and appoint his successor; Rev Howard Knight had been introduced at that farewell meeting. Then there had been the affairs of the Keswick bookshops to settle up, and time had to be taken for much-needed surgery. While he was recovering in hospital he had written a small book which had been commissioned by the IVF. He really had not thought this last task could have been managed, but not so Edith! He laughed as he recalled how she would not let him 'off the hook'. 'You promised!' she said, and so it had been fitted in along with all that was involved in selling their home and buying a smaller one where Wilbur, within a few weeks of his eighteenth birthday and in his final year at school, was to live with Oswald's niece, Beryl Ford.

There had barely been time to settle the matters of real estate. The final transaction was only signed at a quarter to five on Friday, 20 August, and they had to leave Melbourne the following Monday! It was almost as though God had put His seal upon the matter saying, 'There, I've stamped it for you!'

Then there had been final meetings in Adelaide and Perth, and now he was facing Singapore where he must begin to come to grips with his new job.

It was not going to be easy either for him or for the

various councils with whom he had to work, because the terms of reference for the position of the new General Director were so different from those relating to his four predecessors. They, in close consultation with all other Directors, had been responsible for the work of the Mission at all levels. Oswald would be the first General Director who would be required to delegate all matters directly relating to the fields to the Overseas Director. His own responsibilities, apart from liaison between the home countries and the fields, might appear to be rather nebulous. Too nebulous in the view of some, particularly the London council. Obviously the job would become largely what the General Director made of it. But right then he was being thrown in at the deep end, and he had no idea what shoals might lie beneath the surface. He had so much to learn!

Because there had been no General Director for three years it was going to be imperative that he should be seen and recognised by all members of the Mission. In view of the great changes on the field, there were urgent matters to be discussed with all the home councils. It was going to mean travel – much travel.

As he contemplated the coming months he could thank God that on this initial journey at least he would have Edith's companionship. She had brushed up her secretarial skills and so would be able to act as his secretary. But he knew that most of all he would value her support. Shy and unsure of himself beneath that calm exterior, he found that moving constantly from one new situation to another was not easy, and it never became easy. Edith would act as his ice-breaker. Though shy herself, she yet had a quiet dignity and a ready smile that won a warm response wherever she went. Looking back years later he said simply, 'I'd have been sunk without her.'

Of the three crowded weeks in Singapore Edith wrote

to an inner circle of family and friends that for Oswald 'every hour has been more than needed for him to get a correct picture of all the fields and their needs and problems, and likewise the home departments . . . His needs are deep and big.'

Then she summed up a vivid account of an exhaustive and exhausting tour in the Malay States with the observation: 'We were struck by the various forms the enemy's opposition takes. We visited ten villages in two days, travelling hard . . . talking while we ate . . . hearing of their hopes and fears . . . Almost without exception, especially where there had been fruit, . . . the enemy hit right into the centre of the work. No wonder one lady said she found it difficult to maintain an attitude of expectancy.' The battle was joined; and Oswald never forgot it during the years ahead.

They sailed for Europe on 2 October. Those were still the days of the 'boat people', before jet air travel became either common or relatively cheap, so most missionaries still travelled by sea or overland. Although the three weeks from Singapore to Genoa may have afforded some relaxation after the pace of the previous months, Oswald always found sea travel boring. He was to be glad when later the sheer demands of time were to make air travel a necessity. Even jet-lag was not to worry him; he found he could largely ignore it! He sympathises with those who suffer from it, but for himself, 'The Lord has given me quick recuperative powers; another legacy from my mother. Although she was not robust she always seemed able to rally her strength for special demands.' In his mid-eighties he still jets calmly from one series of meetings to another. But he does make the concession of not attempting to do much on long flights!

From Genoa they travelled into Switzerland, and Edith, in her letters to a small, intimate group, sought to draw 'the dear ones at home' close to her as she wrote of the delights of travelling in that lovely country. These letters, long, detailed and unhurried, in spite of the pace of her life, reveal her own humble enjoyment of world travel as one of God's 'extras' that were added to what was often a stressful way of life for her. As for Oswald, in spite of the tiring necessity of speaking through an interpreter, he was always to enjoy Switzerland: its serene beauty; its Bible colleges full of eager students; and its churches with their keen missionary thrust and overflowing generosity to the cause of missions.

But within a fortnight they were on their way to London and Oswald could be only too aware of the difference between this visit and the two previous occasions. Then he had been welcomed by his friend, Fred Mitchell. This time he would have to make his own way. True enough, on those visits he had met most if not all of the London council members. But then he had come representing small home countries 'down under'; he had posed no threat. Now, he was all too conscious of his vastly different role, and of the prime necessity of winning their acceptance right from the start. There were two marks against him: one, the fact that he had had no field experience; the other that he was a 'colonial'. But they must have been reassured by his unassuming manner, combined with a dignified bearing, an excellent voice and an astute mind. In spite of his inner misgivings, they saw only a man who was humbly confident in his God.

In the event, he was to find that the London council was much more concerned lest the decisions of the Bournemouth conference three years earlier may have resulted in some weakening of the office of General Director. The London council of those days saw themselves as very much the senior council, successors to that original body that had been established in Hudson Taylor's day, in 1865 when the Mission had been founded. As such they held themselves to be guardians of those hallowed traditions, and jealous as they were of their own position, they were yet more jealous for the office that had once been held by Hudson Taylor. Just how serious was the threat posed by vesting the oversight of field matters in the office of the Overseas Director? Oswald sought to reassure them that his own portfolio would keep him more than fully occupied, but some remained only half convinced.

He was also to learn that it was important to understand how each of the councils in the different home countries saw its own role. It was small wonder, for instance, that the North American councils should resent any hint of seniority or interference on the part of the London council. They had their own hallowed traditions, and apart from national differences, each represented different groups of churches with different emphases within a common evangelical basis. It was to call forth all his administrative skills and much prayerful diplomacy. At least the North Americans saw his 'colonial' status as making him one with themselves! They may well have resented a Britisher who came to them without the prior qualification of field service. Indeed there had been occasions when they had not been altogether happy with Bishop Houghton's administration as far as it affected them. The General Director of an international and interdenominational mission must learn to walk a very fine line! Again and again Oswald was to come to the point of despair wondering, 'Who is sufficient for all these things?' And then how good it was to lean back hard on the fact that the responsibility was God's, and He *was* adequate. It was to be the only way he could cope.

While in London on this occasion, Oswald took the opportunity of calling on Dr Martyn Lloyd-Jones of Westminster Chapel, who was at that time a member of the OMF council. The doctor welcomed the opportunity to talk on a personal basis, and on learning of Oswald's Welsh background, exclaimed that 'somewhere along the line the "u" must have been dropped from' his family name; 'Saunders' being the usual Welsh version.

It was pleasant to forget about pressures of time as they talked at length, exchanging views on matters of wide-ranging importance, and enjoying real fellowship of mind and spirit. Oswald needed such friendships which he was to make in a number of places as his travels continued. They stretched his mind and opened windows on the current evangelical scene. The understanding gained through such contacts, added to his already considerable experience, helped to prepare him to lead the Mission through crises that lay ahead. The Overseas Director, Arnold Lea, was to see Oswald's ability both to speak and to write on a broad range of topics as being one of God's good gifts to the OMF. That ability was soon to be recognised across the broad spectrum of evangelical missions.

Meanwhile, the relentless pace of the itinerary swept him on, and by December he had crossed the Atlantic by sea to commence a tour that would take him and Edith all over Canada and the United States. Soon after their arrival in Philadelphia, he received an urgent telegram: Could he take the place of one of the main speakers at the Urbana Student Missionary Convention between Christmas and New Year? His schedule was full; the topics would require careful and specific preparation, and he could not see where or how he could get the necessary reference books. It was an impossibility. 'That doesn't take much praying about!' was his comment to Edith. 'But *have* you prayed about it?' was her disconcerting reply.

Well, of course he hadn't prayed about it, but it seemed that he should. So he sat down with pencil and paper and began to think. The topics were: 'The first hundred years of missions' and 'The last one hundred and fifty years of missions', and he began to jot down the names of books he considered would be essential for reference. There were six, and most if not all were out of print. So there was the basis of his prayer: immediate access to all six would be necessary before he could begin to cope with the assignment. It would take a small miracle and that seemed impossible. This was another way in which he sometimes sought guidance. By reducing a matter to its essential elements and simply laying them before God, it cleared the mind of nebulous thought and then it was often possible to see in which direction God was pointing.

He was in the city of Grand Rapids and next day he had to go and interview the manager of a large firm of Christian publishers on some OMF matters. On the way there he recollected that this firm also had the biggest second-hand book department in the country, and he began to wonder. So, his primary business concluded, he told the manager of his problem. What were the books in question? Oswald took out his list, naming the books one by one. Yes, they had that – and that – and also that one – and so through the list of six! They were all there on the shelves! The small miracle had happened and the way was clear ahead. It opened the door for him into the remarkable Urbana Student Missionary Conference that was beginning to bring the cause of missions to the forefront of the minds of an ever-increasing number of students.

After Urbana he was glad to share in the intimacy of a conference for OMF home staff members and to get to know them as individuals behind the names in the prayer list. They on their part learned to know him as a leader who could open the word of God and from it speak to their specific needs, then quite naturally pass on to leading their discussions through knotty points of administration. Quickly his sharp mind seized upon the snag at the heart of a problem, guiding them surely towards its unravelling.

The whirlwind schedule of meetings continued to carry him all over North America, until even he was glad to embark on the *SS United States* for the return to England. They knew no one among the 2,000 passengers and, oh, the relief of relaxing into the blessed privacy of anonymity, enjoying their comfortable cabin and table for two in a quiet corner of the dining room!

The weather was kind to them. After only a couple of days' rest Oswald was ready for work again and, as Edith wrote, 'to see visions and begin preparation for the work awaiting him in England'. Many meetings and much unfinished work had still to be dealt with. What few people guessed at was all the correspondence which Edith described as 'mountainous' that lay on his desk at every OMF centre. As his secretary she would quietly reduce it to order before he started on it, often late at night after meetings and interviews were over. She marvelled at the strength given him to cope, but gave little hint of what such pressured times cost her.

Edith returned alone to Singapore while Oswald was thankful to follow by plane. He needed to arrive in time to prepare for the next session of the overseas council to begin on 17 May 1955 – the first since his appointment as General Director.

The previous long, crammed eight months had been a continuous learning experience for him and it continued through the fortnight of the council, and on through visits around six of the fields where he gave addresses at their council meetings, right up to the end of that year.

Moreover the pace of those months was to prove to be the pattern for the next fifteen years. Those periods when his diary schedule indicates that he stayed in Singapore for several months at a stretch were even more pressured. They were periods when the Overseas Director was away from the field and Oswald had perforce to wear two hats! He looks back almost in disbelief that he could have come through those periods of immense strain. In later years, after Oswald's retirement, extra provision was made to ease the burden during the absence of the Overseas Director. The wonder is that he did not crack under the strain.

Only the long-established practice of early rising, and the strictly-disciplined use of his time, which included retiring at a reasonable hour, enabled him to cope with it. Years before, at the Bible college, Les Rushbrook had observed his ability to give himself wholly to the task in hand and then, at need, to switch off and put it right out of his mind while he dealt with the demands of the next moment. Doubtless his legal training and well-disciplined mind played a considerable part in this, but there must also have been some innate gift that, fully yielded back to the One who had given it, was used to the utmost by Him in His service. And Oswald found that with every fresh burden there was fresh grace given for whatever the day might hold. While he never ceased to be keenly conscious of his own inadequacy, he was entirely satisfied with the sufficiency of Christ, longing only that he might be able to appropriate to the full, all the grace there was for him in Christ.

II. YOUR FLOCK OF GOD

'It was not so much because of his gifts that we appreciated him; it was most of all because of his willingness to help us.' Such was Arnold Lea's summing up, fifteen years later, of the years of Oswald's leadership. No accolade could have satisfied him more than that. 'See

that your "flock of God" is properly fed and cared for,'
had been the specific terms of God's commission. It was
the task to which from the first he gave the highest
priority. In all Edith's letters the paramount thought is
the longing that Oswald – that they both – should be
blessed only so that blessing should flow out in every
situation.

No one is an easier target for Satan's darts than a
missionary wearied by months and years of coping with
a difficult climate, a strange language and culture,
loneliness and discouragement. Centuries earlier,
Samuel Rutherford, that rugged Scot who was forbidden
by the authorities to preach anywhere in Scotland, had
penned hundreds of letters full of spiritual pith and verve
to brace the spirits of his scattered flock. 'Faith is the
better of . . . the sharp winter storm in its face,' he wrote
in one of those letters. 'Grace withers without adversity,'
he continued. 'The devil is but God's master fencer to
teach us to handle our weapons.' So now Oswald, often
using a Bible character to press home his point, spoke
and sometimes wrote to his fellow missionaries. All were
men and women for whom he had a profound regard; as
those who had chosen to walk with God in obscure and
difficult paths, they merited only the best that he could
offer. When at times it might seem that his counsel
contained more of astringency than of soothing balm, it
was because he knew that the warfare in which they were
engaged called for strong spiritual muscle tone.

A veteran field leader was at first surprised at
Oswald's response when one day he remarked how
much he would like to sit back and enjoy some good
Bible teaching. Oswald looked at him: 'Well, you're old
enough to forage for yourself, aren't you?' was all he said.
Did he not understand the man's need? A need common
to all who are called upon to be constantly giving out
physically, mentally and emotionally. Of course he

understood and deeply sympathised. But he also knew that it was an essential prerequisite that every missionary should be able to dig for his own daily food from the word of God. Moreover, he knew his man; he knew him as one who had within himself deep spiritual resources upon which he could draw as leader and encourager of others. Certainly Percy Moore never forgot that bracing reminder that nerved him to years of fresh endeavour.

Nor did he ever forget Oswald's encouragement on another occasion when he was hesitating about taking a difficult decision that concerned another missionary: 'Grasp the nettle and get on with it! It's the only way!' was Oswald's salutary advice. And it was advice that not only Percy Moore but other field leaders gratefully followed.

Yet it was not to be expected that all missionaries would find Oswald easy to approach. 'Austere' was a word commonly used of him during that period. All were aware of his stern self-disciplines and were often equally aware of their own shortcomings, so that they tended to see in him something of an Olympian detachment. Probably none guessed that it was a cover-up for his own acute sense of insufficiency for his task as leader. Certainly it is very doubtful if any guessed at his underlying shyness, any more than those who served under Winston Churchill could have guessed that under his bombast lay an essentially shy nature. Most of us do not expect leaders to be shy.

It was during one of those pressured periods when he had to wear two hats, his own and the Overseas Director's, that a young lady came to see him. 'As Overseas Director, J O S remained approachable, sympathetic, the opposite of austere and formidable,' she recalls. 'When I asked for permission to visit Saiburi Hospital as part of my holiday, J O S's response was to send me there for two weeks *prior* to my holiday, to get back in touch with medicine.' Oswald knew how to encourage keen young workers!

Some time later, when she became engaged to be married, she was surprised and delighted when he took the time to write a warm letter of good wishes to them both. She was further impressed when after a considerable period of time he recognised them at a chance encounter and remembered their names. He has always been remarkable for his ability to remember faces and names, and such detailed concern is certainly not born of detachment, especially when his general dislike of detail is remembered.

Edith used to say that the Lord knew what He was about when He gave both Arnold Lea and Oswald wives who were less than robust. It was so that they could better understand the needs of women in the fellowship! An older worker, advised by the doctor that she should delay her return to the field for a few months, was concerned lest that might mean doing other work that would create further pressures. 'No,' said Oswald. 'You have nothing at all to do but to get well!' And with that positive encouragement she was able to do just that.

Even so, his real forte lay not so much in dealing with individuals as in speaking to groups, large or small. Each field held its own conference of missionaries every year or so, when future strategies were planned, and a closely-knit team spirit was fostered. The most important element was the time of unhurried devotion spent together each day, led by a visiting speaker, often one of the Directors. Oswald was the speaker at no less than six of these conferences in what remained of that incredible year of learning in 1954–55. His messages were no mere trite homilies. They brought the relevance of the word of God right into the towns or villages, the lonely mountainsides, or the teeming cities where these men and women spent their lives. They were messages full of common sense that took their varied circumstances into account.

He began to get first-hand glimpses of those circumstances when he took occasion on these visits to spend some time in as many centres as possible. Staying in their homes he observed, he listened, he learned. A quiet, helpful guest, it was obvious to all that he looked for no red carpet treatment, and small children responded happily to his gentle approach. He was welcomed wherever he went and especially when Edith accompanied him.

Women in inland field centres, often isolated and working in stressful situations of one kind or another, appreciated her warm interest in their problems. They appreciated, too, her simple but attractive style of dress. The perfectionist in her always dressed carefully. 'She's good for us,' they said. 'She keeps us from getting slack.'

And in some subtle, unconscious way she often interpreted her husband to some who might find him difficult to approach. She had certainly achieved this for students on those early visits to the Katoomba and Upwey Conventions in Australia and she continued to do so in her new role. Moreover, during the quite considerable period that she spent in Singapore, often when Oswald was away, she demonstrated her versatility by 'filling in' on a number of different tasks. And always she made a vital contribution to the happiness of the International Headquarters compound.

In a remarkably short time both Oswald and Edith found themselves warmly welcomed into the heart of the OMF family that was to come to mean so much to them both. Missionaries began to turn eagerly to the General Director's letter that appeared unfailingly in each issue of their in-house bulletin. Long, warm and thought-provoking, these letters seemed able to reach out and draw them all closer together in their common task. If, as well, his name appeared above an article on some current topic, then that was an added bonus. They began to thank God for his strong, articulate leadership, and rejoiced when they saw his wide ministry spilling over to student conferences and Christian conventions throughout the world.

Thus gradually, with the passage of time, Oswald began to understand something of God's purpose in calling him to the task. The times and circumstances were such that they called for a good deal of adaptability. The whole Mission situation was in a state of flux as it adapted to the new fields, and the further it progressed along its new path, the more obvious it was that it could not look only to past precedents for reference along its future way. A leader whose active experience had lain almost wholly within the sphere of the mission field, would hardly have been prepared for all the fresh demands that were to be made upon the new General Director.

At last Oswald was able to see that God was using all his previous experience, in law practice, in business, in the Bible college and in general ministry, along with a certain natural versatility, to equip him for the task to which God had so clearly called him.

10

Sharing Leadership

All through the years of the Mission's history God has called into its service many men and women of exceptional gifts and qualifications, and at the commencement of Oswald's leadership there were within its ranks leaders of outstanding ability who had helped to steady it through the crises of the last years in China and into the commencement of work in the new fields. They were the men whose invitation to join them as their General Director had so astounded him. So in joining them none recognised more clearly than he that it would not be a case of the General Director standing head and shoulders above his fellow directors, but rather of his standing shoulder to shoulder with them as members of a team. Arnold Lea remarked that if sometimes it may have appeared as though Oswald were standing on the touch line, he was certainly not there as a spectator but rather as coach of the team. He was a vital part of the team. Without him they would have lacked cohesion and that vital spark of inspiration that is so essential to good teamwork. It was Arnold Lea, too, who observed that although Oswald did not display a scintillating personality that dazzled on a first meeting, yet, when men rubbed shoulders with him as they bent to their common task, then the solid gold beneath shone through.

It was true that the General Director delegated to the Overseas Director the responsibility for field administration, but it was equally true that the General Director was obliged by the Mission constitution to delegate this authority. It was a situation that could have held seeds of contention, but no such problem arose during the sixteen years that Arnold Lea and Oswald worked together. He knew he had everything to learn about the work on the fields and he was only too willing to leave that responsibility with the Overseas Director. But he watched, he accepted advice, and he learned – he was a quick learner. Arnold Lea recalls that when Oswald joined them he must have thought them 'a rather pedestrian lot'. He had been used to taking quick decisions and seeing them implemented forthwith in the area of his business activities. Now he had to learn to adapt to the all-important family spirit of the Mission; to take full account of the widely differing personalities involved and to proceed more slowly.

As far as he and Arnold Lea were concerned, the two men very soon worked out a thoroughly happy *modus operandi*. They were two very different temperaments but they were equals in godliness and vision. Oswald says of his co-director: 'He was much deeper than I. I'm a more superficial sort of person. I tend to deal with the present problem without concerning myself too much with future outworkings. He would sound the note of caution that would hold me back from acting impulsively.'

For his part, Arnold Lea states positively that he has never worked with anyone who had a more equable disposition than Oswald's. And he learned to appreciate to the full the General Director's qualities as a leader, and his special gifts as a 'front man', ably representing the Mission in the home countries, and maintaining a high profile in all inter-mission affairs.

Nevertheless there were sometimes strong differences

of opinion. It could not have been otherwise. The important factor was not the clash of opinion but the manner in which they handled it. Failure to agree always brought them to their knees. Together and individually they faced it out with God. The Holy Spirit became the Arbiter, and always He brought them to full unity of purpose. They were experiences that must have been wonderfully strengthening and enriching in the life of each man. They were certainly of incalculable blessing in the life of the Mission. Its members were spared the destructive spectacle of its two senior executives vying with one another in matters of implementing Mission policy. Indeed it was not long before the staff at International Headquarters, the body of directors and finally the whole fellowship were thanking God for His provision of these two leaders who complemented each other in such a remarkable way. However, Oswald has always recognised and appreciated that grace of humility with which Arnold Lea, though abundantly qualified to serve as General Director, happily accepted what was officially the position of No 2 in the team.

Then there was the broader aspect of sharing leadership with the whole body of directors. The General Director was free to make decisions of importance only after full consultation with that body. He was plunged into one of these councils in October 1955, only a week after returning from his first marathon tour as General Director. It was a council of field leaders only and so the Overseas Director was in the chair. Oswald insisted that this should always be so, although when the council embraced the Home Directors as well he was very willing to take the chair. Responding to the council's official welcome, he reiterated his consciousness of his serious lack of field experience and emphasised again his readiness to learn. And learn he did.

A minor matter that surfaced during that council

session concerned the constant changes in the prayer directory. In a mission whose membership was numbered in the hundreds and constantly growing, this was inevitable. In the China days the Mission wits had declared that CIM stood for Constantly In Motion! The change to OMF was no problem to them: 'It's Only More Frequently,' they quipped. But the constant directory changes *were* a problem to busy missionaries who often shirked the dreary task in spite of really wanting to keep in touch with each other's movements. Was there no simpler way?

In the discussion that followed, Oswald sought leave to speak: 'Well, Mr Chairman, we all have the same amount of time in a day, and it's all a question of how we organise it!' The tone was brisk, incisive, and there were raised eyebrows and wry smiles. 'He'll learn!' flashed the silent signals.

In the next session of council when Oswald was in the chair, reference was again made to the old chestnut, and someone began to talk about organising time. 'I don't know that it's as simple as that.' The voice from the chair was slower, and it lacked the incisive note. 'As I go around the fields and see the loads missionaries carry, and the conditions under which they work, I realise how little time they have to call their own.' There were appreciative nods and quiet smiles. 'He's learning!' said the signals.

There was something else his quick perceptions picked up during that council session in 1955. He had seen something like it back in 1947 when that marathon China sweep had taken him to a large, isolated and strategic CIM centre. Then he had electrified the missionaries who had asked him to speak at their weekly prayer meeting by announcing that he was going to speak on *What I would do in this compound if I were the devil!* And his shots had found their mark as he targeted in on telling how he would work overtime at sowing discord among those who lived and worked there.

Now he was looking at a group of men who in those China days had enjoyed a very close sense of camaraderie. Apart from their personal loyalty to Christ, there had been the common bond of a love for the Chinese people and their ancient culture and language. Their conversation was frequently laced with picturesque Chinese phrases, and this had generated good humour and a close family spirit.

Moreover, the problems with which they had coped had not been nearly so complex as those which faced them now. Then it had not been so difficult to work out blanket policies to cover their different areas of work. Now it was impossible because their new fields were so diverse. As he watched and listened, Oswald realised that some of these men who were valiantly coping with new and diverse languages, and representing widely different peoples and cultures, had not yet understood that blanket policies were not the answer in these new circumstances. As each man pulled at the inadequate blanket in a determined effort to stretch it to cover the special requirements of 'his' field, tempers became frayed, voices were raised and unity was threatened.

All this Oswald was able to take in almost as an onlooker at the first session of council following his appointment. From his position 'on the touch line' he identified both the practical and the spiritual weak spots in the team work. As to the practical outworking of policies, his keen, analytical mind saw quickly to the heart of these matters, and he was able to begin pointing out the advisability of developing more broadly-based policies that could cover the varying needs.

On the spiritual side he laid his own plans for the future. He was to chair the next council session in November 1956 and when the agenda was being drawn up he suggested that all delegates from the fields and home countries should gather in Singapore by the Saturday prior to the opening of the session, so that the Sunday could be spent as a day of retreat. The days in council would be long and pressured, but that first day together would be one of unhurried worship and fellowship around the word of God. Martin Luther had once said when facing a heavy day's programme: 'I have so much to do that I shall spend the first three hours in prayer.' And as those men, fresh from situations dominated by the urgent, put aside questions that clamoured for resolution, they found themselves relaxing into the peace of God. It was a never to be forgotten day when they drew so close to each other and to their Lord that in the busy days that followed tempers did not become frayed nor were voices raised in anger. That quiet day became established practice, the eagerly anticipated highlight of future sessions of council.

Given the calibre of the men gathered for those councils, it was not surprising that not all of Oswald's ideas were immediately accepted. Nor was it surprising that he did not relish their rejection. But he was too wise to press a point; he merely bided his time, and it is significant that more often than not, those ideas were eventually adopted.

One important issue for which he never succeeded in gaining acceptance concerned the greater participation of women in the leadership of the Mission. And in this case it was remarkable that the main opposition came from women themselves who were not then ready for it. Now, more than twenty years on, he has the satisfaction of seeing a woman on the Directorate at International Headquarters.

During his term of office several issues arose within the Christian church worldwide that in one way or another deeply affected the life and work of the Mission. One of those was the upsurge of the charismatic movement. As evangelicals drawn from churches of different denominations, including some with charismatic connections, the members of the fellowship lived in harmony with one another, respecting each other's viewpoints. When, therefore, some missionaries returning from furlough sought to impose charismatic views upon others, some action had to be taken. Then one man mailed a long, anonymous circular to the entire membership urging extreme charismatic views. There was some agitation in the Fellowship ranks that all affected should be asked to resign, but Arnold Lea counselled caution. Oswald continues the story: 'I went to the field affected and conferred with the whole missionary body. After discussion I laid down the guidelines of Mission policy on the matter. They were reasonable and acceptable to the great majority. A few, who had adopted a very militant attitude and were unwilling to follow the guidelines and abandon their potentially divisive attitude, withdrew from the fellowship. But the crisis passed.' The simple statement gives no hint of the personal cost involved; of the deep heart searching; of the sleepless nights during the months that he and Arnold Lea had agonised over the matter. Looking back, Arnold Lea recalled that Oswald had dealt with the situation 'with strong hands but with those wearing gloves'. But it was certainly the patient, conciliatory approach on the part of its two leaders that saved the Fellowship from a deeply divisive split.

Another situation involved the writing of a difficult letter. One of the home churches that supported a couple on one of the fields learned that in another country OMF had several workers involved in Bible teaching ministries in a national church affiliated with the World Council of Churches. The Mission had no such affiliation, but the home church concerned objected to even this distant 'connection' and firmly stated that they could no longer support OMF unless they withdrew their workers from those churches. Oswald did not feel the objection was valid, but he and Arnold Lea discussed it with fellow-directors. They concluded that 'guilt by association' was a questionable concept. To refuse meant the loss of two valuable workers who themselves did not wish to leave the Mission. On the other hand compliance would mean deliberately closing a door which they believed God had opened. It would mean withdrawing workers from strategic roles in leadership training, Bible teaching, training of Sunday school teachers and preparing material for their use. It would mean leaving this field wide open to those holding liberal theological views. Surely it would be going back on guidance. And so Oswald had to write one of the most difficult letters of his life. 'Letters are an unsatisfactory means of communication,' he writes in his book *Spiritual Leadership*. 'They cannot smile when they are saying something difficult, and therefore additional care should be taken to see that they are warm in tone.' But that letter came from a heavy heart.

A third matter concerned the Revised Standard Version of the Bible. The publication of the whole Bible in this version in 1952 stirred up a storm of protest in evangelical circles regarding its translation of certain passages. Ultimately, not long after Oswald had assumed office, the USA Director received a letter from a generous supporter asking several questions as to the attitude of OMF to the RSV. As the Mission had no policy for or against the RSV, but left it to the individual missionary, the Director consulted Oswald who was in the USA at the time.

The letter indicated that if the Mission continued to use the RSV it would mean the withdrawal of financial support – a matter of $132,000 annually, a considerable amount of money at that time, and the Mission could not really afford to lose such a large slice of its income. Oswald was staggered at what was involved. He knew that all members would exercise care with regard to the passages in question, but neither he nor the directorate had the right to enter into an agreement that would preclude their ever being able to use the RSV. Not that Oswald himself was unable to appreciate the godly zeal that lay behind the demands. He had grown up among many such men in New Zealand and they had helped to mould his early thinking. Moreover he was appalled at the thought of the cost to missionaries on the field. But he authorised that letter of refusal, again drawing flak towards himself personally. Then he and the Mission treasurer and other directors committed their need to God, and in the long run Mission income did not suffer.

That decision accorded well with his own firmly-held belief concerning finance as it relates to the work of God: 'The policy I have believed and adhered to is that finance should not be the deciding factor in any decision regarding spiritual work. It should be *a* factor but it should not be the deciding factor. I have never been money-hungry, believing that we should be just as willing to receive less as more.' He learned to appreciate the value of money, especially during the great depression of the thirties. As far as he is concerned, having 'more' means not just greater comfort for himself, but also a greater capacity to enjoy the pleasure of sharing with others.

On the positive side was a highlight in the Mission's history that was to have far-reaching implications for the future of the work. Not that it was Oswald's brain-child; the seeds of the idea had been lying dormant for some time. It related to the developing concern for world mission within the fast-maturing churches of East Asia. At first the OMF could not see what their response should be. To form a parallel body for Asians would only emphasise differences between east and west. But one night after he had spoken at a student missionary gathering in Singapore, fifteen young people said they wanted to become missionaries. How could they go about it? There was no sending group to whom he could refer them. Then one evening shortly afterwards, he found these eager young Chinese students on the steps leading to his flat. How could they become involved in world mission? And Oswald was embarrassed to have so little to offer them. Not long after, when he was in Japan, the same question arose in conversations with pastors there, and in after-meetings in which a hundred young Japanese offered themselves for missionary service. Evidently the Holy Spirit was moving and the OMF must be alert to catch His direction.

And so, after many months of careful thought and prayer, Oswald came to the central council of October 1964 convinced that it was time for the Mission to make a decisive forward move in this area. He anticipated some deeply entrenched opposition, but he counted on God to enable him to lead his colleagues towards that same vision which occupied his own mind. The outworking of its realisation was still not clear to him, but for that, too, he was counting on God. From the chair he presented his challenge:

'We meet at an apocalyptic hour in world history and at a point of crisis and great potentiality in the annals of the Mission. So great have been the changes in the last two decades that unless we can adopt a more contemporary and progressive stance . . . we are going to lose ground.'

Dr Jim Broomhall had written a paper on Asians and the Fellowship. Up to that point they had, in Arnold Lea's words, 'been stumbling about in the dark.' But this paper proved to be the watershed, indicating future directions. In retrospect it seems to have indicated an obvious solution. But nearly a quarter of a century ago it was not so obvious. In essence the idea set out was that the OMF should change from being a western body serving in eastern fields, to become a meld of eastern and western Christians in a new fellowship where workers of all nationalities should serve together, with their own home councils, with the same financial policy of looking to God for funds, and pooling all financial resources. It was such a revolutionary concept at that time that there was initial hesitation. But Oswald encouraged debate and a full airing of views. He himself had prepared a paper on the subject, and as the discussion continued he realised that it needed some clarification. So while the discussion flowed around him he rewrote certain sections. Arnold Lea recalls that as the days of council continued, the subject 'was gradually hammered out on the anvil of debate and slowly took shape as J O S skilfully guided us towards the decision that would have to be made, and step by step we followed him'.

It was very significant that that tremendous issue was introduced, debated, and the motion formally tabled and implemented all within that one session of council. 'I feel that one of his great contributions to the Mission,' says Arnold Lea, 'was this ability to get things on paper, then challenge people to face up to the implications and make a decision. Things could not be left in the air as far as Oswald was concerned.' And on that occasion he brought his final challenge: 'If we could see the way through, it would not be a step of faith. Did Hudson Taylor see the way through when he took that first mighty step of faith? His eyes were on the Lord, not on the way stretching at his feet . . . God is calling us to go forward, what is your response?'

Unanimously they agreed that it was a God-given vision. A vision that has grown clearer and stronger over the years of its realisation, when the outstanding factor has been the very high calibre of the Asian men and women who have joined the fellowship as field workers and as home council members.

Looking back on those years of Mission leadership, Oswald smiles ruefully when he admits he has not been able to measure up to the high standards he himself set out in his book *Spiritual Leadership*. But he was welcomed by other leaders in the Mission because of his readiness to listen to suggestions; and to delegate authority even when he would rather not. Merciless in his demands upon himself, he could make allowances for a man going through a rough patch. When letters began to come in from a field complaining that the leader was falling down on his job, some even suggesting he should be removed from office, he and Arnold Lea talked it over. But they received no clear guidance. Then Oswald suggested they follow his practical method and that each should make his own list of pros and cons. When they compared lists they found that on both of them the number of pros for allowing the man to continue far outnumbered the cons. That man battled through the bad patch to years of further service.

And Oswald was an encourager. He once spent a Saturday afternoon driving a newcomer to Headquarters to all the points of interest in Singapore 'just to get his mind working'. He could be devastatingly frank when occasion demanded that he should point out areas of weakness. But 'you got in straight from the shoulder, and you got it all; you knew there was nothing more and you knew that was the end of it'.

Oswald often says, 'God gives you a good nose for people!' And during his time as General Director he made some noteworthy appointments, but not all of his choices, or rejections, were received wholeheartedly. It may have been that what he saw as a lack of any other option precipitated an error of judgement. Or it may have been one of those occasions when he failed to see the long-term implications. Whatever the reason it could mean hurt or a sense of let-down for someone. He was not infallible and he knew it – he was human.

But in sharing leadership, his colleagues found him to be dependable, remarkably even-tempered; a man who never seemed to be at his wit's end; a man who was serenely confident – not in his particular gifts and abilities – but only in his God.

11

The Cost of Leadership

The year 1964 which closed on such a high note for the Mission had opened on a period of increasing difficulty for Oswald and Edith. They were neither of them well. For ten years Oswald had been driving himself hard, while Edith had striven to keep pace in her own sphere. They were years of inevitable physical, mental and nervous strain. Many years later Oswald talked informally of one aspect of those years of leadership, the decisions concerning other people:

> Those are the most difficult of all decisions, because the people concerned are your friends. You must weigh up the interests of the work against your natural feelings for your friends, although the two are not to be entirely dissociated. But I found all decisions relating to people's lives, and in particular any disciplinary decision, *very* hard; I had to screw myself up to do it. If only those people who feel you are being tough on them could know the genuine agony of heart you go through before you come to a decision, they'd have a different viewpoint on it. I found that very, very costly. You can't divulge confidences and give all the reasons, you just have to take the knock. Well, that's what you're there for! But it doesn't make it any easier. It's hard when your motivation is misunderstood; when you're really acting in the best interests of the individual and they can't see it. They

can only see administrative toughness. But I found this – the situation doesn't improve with age. The longer you leave it, the more difficult it becomes. Once you've done your homework; made thorough inquiries into both sides; and got all the facts that are relevant so that you can get an objective appraisal of the situation, then deal with it at once.

Get it over with! Otherwise you will have days and nights of fruitless agony, and still you will have to do it. *And* – if you do reach a decision and then go back on it, you're generally wrong. Not always, but generally. Once allow your heart to rule your head, and give the person the benefit of the doubt, it very seldom works out. You can try to inject some comfort into the decision; you can deal with it as gently as possible and make your reasons as clear as possible, but generally they are not able to listen to those things; they can only hear the decision.

That was one of the reasons why I didn't want to take on the job. I knew too well what it would involve; what I would have to carry; because by the time a decision reaches your desk, the buck stops. And it wouldn't get to your desk unless it was a difficult decision. It takes real moral courage to make such decisions, and again and again I found it hard to summon up that courage.

'He does carry a very heavy load and I know it does, in one sense, press on his spirit . . . You can't carry burdens without cost.' So runs one of Edith's letters. And again, 'Sometimes personnel problems come in pretty thick, for we have a big family. There are heartaches when casualties occur, and always heart-searching lest the cause has been failure on our part.'

Furthermore, it was all in the context of the jet age that burst upon the world at about the time that Oswald took office, so that he was the Mission's first General Director to live at such a pace. It meant that often he was, so to speak, hurled from one crisis to another, hundreds, even thousands, of miles away, with almost no time to relax in between. It called for all the resilience of mind and spirit ·

he could muster. He knew he should take time off for much-needed surgery, but the constant, inexorable demands of a tight schedule meant that he kept on regardless.

Along with all this he had been troubled by a neuritic condition in his heels. It had begun soon after his arrival in Singapore and the acute pain had taken its own nervous toll in a lifestyle such as his. Several doctors made various suggestions for relief, from gentle exercise to vitamins and emollients, but it continued. Dr John Laird, with his own brand of sanctified common sense, suggested more sleep and regular holidays! Advice which Oswald and Edith tried to follow, but more often than not found it to be impossible. Eventually a podiatrist in Seattle, Dr Sewell, devised a support that gave a good deal of relief.

But it was Edith's health that was causing the greatest concern. Oswald had deliberately tried to protect her from highly emotive issues and she herself asked that he should not tell her everything 'so that people can't winkle it out of me'. Even so, because she so often acted as his secretary, it was inevitable that she should learn of things that distressed her. Dr Laird thought it possible that Oswald 'may not have understood fully how hard it was for Edith to keep up with her husband's enormous energy and creative activity'.

Oswald himself says simply, 'I think I probably asked too much of her.' And while that may be so, it was not as simple as that. Edith was one of life's givers. She gave eagerly, with both hands, and it was her joy to give of herself in her role at Oswald's side. The perfectionist in her would have been frustrated with a lesser involvement. But because she had always distrusted her own gifts and abilities, she looked constantly to Oswald to nudge her on. It was little wonder then that after nearly ten years she was exhausted. 'The fill-gap jobs ran me right out nervously,' she wrote in January 1964. 'We are ready to spend and be spent for the Lord, but perhaps we haven't been wise in the expenditure, beyond income, of human reserves' . . . 'Oswald is in need of surgery too, and since the directors would not accept his resignation, it has been decreed that we have health leave for a few months. Apparently I must settle for a limited schedule, and we are to try to make our contribution from Australia. Oswald will continue his work as General Director, but with Melbourne as a base instead of Singapore.'

They arrived in Melbourne in March and after a few weeks of rest with their family they were soon settled in a house which Oswald had been able to buy, not far from the OMF centre. Edith began consultations with a psychiatrist, a Christian woman who was able to help her considerably, and Oswald's health was greatly restored after two successive operations. Indeed before the end of September he had regained his amazing energy and was able to return to Singapore where he gave such a strong lead at the October council meetings.

It was 1965, the year of the Mission's centenary, and Oswald was in great demand in the home countries as speaker at special celebrations. Many people were still vague and doubtful about the New Instrument that had been forged during the October council. So this was a golden opportunity to bring to home staff and supporters the challenge of the vision for the new century that had climaxed those council meetings. It would involve a long itinerary, and Edith's health seemed so much better that in faith they went ahead and made bookings for her to set out with Oswald early in June, for North America, Britain and Europe. But while in North America it was evident that she who had delighted to be her husband's ice-breaker, could no longer face those journeys. Oswald had to bring her back to Melbourne and continue alone.

He continued to fill his overseas engagements as General Director, returning to Melbourne as often as possible, until the first half of the following year. Then the final blow fell. Edith had cancer. It was inoperable.

Oswald could hardly take it in, but he had to break it to Edith. That was the most painful nettle he had ever grasped. 'For me, the bottom had dropped out of everything, but when I went to tell Edith she didn't turn a hair. "Oh, I didn't think it was as bad as that." That was all; no sign of panic. Later she said, "When first you told me there was a flicker of fear, but it didn't last long. Then there was a great sense of relief when I realised that I can just lie back in the Lord's arms; I don't have to fight against weakness any more."'

One of the OMF secretaries in Melbourne at the time remembers the shock that swept through the Mission when the doctor's prognosis became known: 'I was seated at the desk just inside the office door when I was dismayed to see JO coming across the courtyard. What did one say – what *could* one say – to such a man at such a time?' She was still speechless when he passed her. But he stopped and turning to her said, 'I know what you're thinking; I know what you want to say.' Then continued on into the inner office.

Oswald has shared the amazing experience of the remaining three months: 'The only way I can express it is that both of us were lifted above sorrow. It was not that we were not acutely aware of the situation; but alongside that there was such a sense of the Lord's presence and support that is indescribable, and it lasted right through. She was really radiant, and never complained.'

Both Oswald and Edith had supreme faith in the power of God to heal in answer to the prayers of His servants, and they had seen Him do this for those for whom they had prayed. But neither of them had the assurance that this was to be God's will on this occasion and acceptance brought with it perfect peace.

Dame Cicely Saunders, founder of the modern Hospice Movement, has this to say of such situations:

> To talk of accepting death when its approach has become inevitable is not mere resignation on the part of the patient nor defeatism on the part of the doctor . . . for both of them it is the very opposite of doing nothing. The patient may well achieve more in this part of his life than in any other, making of it a real reconciliation and fulfilment. This will do more than anything else to comfort the relatives and help them on the road to normal living again.[1]

These words convey a little of the positive value of those months for Edith and Oswald. Edith was able to meet each day with eagerness, even with joy. Her bed was placed in a bright room where Oswald had his desk and with his sister Rita's help and visits from a district nurse, he cared for her constantly, carrying her to and from the bathroom for bathing. The room was a constant bower of flowers from friends all round the world. When Oswald remarked as he drew back the curtains on one of Melbourne's grey winter mornings, 'I'm afraid there will be no sunshine today.' 'Well, we'll create our own,' came the gallant reply, 'and then we will have sunshine!' When she found the going hard: 'I could have felt depressed this morning, but I don't want anyone to see me less than triumphant.'

Right to the last she fought against her temptation to be over-particular: 'I must not stop growing; I must not get fussy near the end; I must check that.' Or again, with

---

[1] *Cicely Saunders – A biography* by Shirley Du Boulay. Hodder Christian Paperbacks.

a note of wonder: 'The Lord has even taken away my sense of failure!'

'It's a wonderful thing to have learned the lesson of trust thoroughly.'

Right at the beginning of that period she told Oswald that she understood that he was going to need another life-partner, and that she was confident that God would lead him. And then she gave herself to setting everything in order – preparing his clothes for his eventual return to Singapore.

Perhaps most amazing of all was the sense of fun that continued to sparkle through even some of the darker moments. Towards the end there was increasing pain and discomfort with recurrent dry-retching, and one day, after an exhausting bout, she popped the empty bowl on her head, and looking up with a wry smile, she said, 'What's the use?' Small wonder that as the nurse was leaving the house one day she turned to Oswald with tears in her eyes. 'How I wish I could take your wife with me when I visit other cancer patients!' she said.

Towards the end of that period, while her strength remained, she wrote him a letter which she gave into Rita's care. Oswald found it on his pillow after he returned from the funeral. It was a beautiful love-letter that dwelt on the positives:

We have reached thirty-five years of cloudless love together . . . You led me into a full, fragrant service, introducing me to such a wealth of dear friends and rich service . . . I have counted it my highest privilege to be in this yoke-service with you and the dear OMF family . . . For what these precious days back at home together have meant, I can never express my thanks or tell you what your surrounding love (and Rita's too) has meant. My life has been a pool of quiet sweetness, and to abide in His love has been made so easy for me – so I abide permanently in God Himself with all the treasures that brings.

My great prayer is that you will be enriched by that which is taken away, that you will be able to make magnificent bouquets out of the refusals of God.

And so in triumph on a Sunday afternoon, 25 September 1966 she passed quietly into the fulness of her Saviour's presence.

Oswald laid her to rest with quiet dignity. Then there followed inevitably that appalling gap and the almost overwhelming sense of loss and desolation.

Scarcely anyone saw that grief. It was too deep, too poignant. Nevertheless in the months ahead back on the fields, friends sensed his 'lostness' and grieved for him.

The following year he was in Japan with Michael Griffiths[1] who was later to succeed him as General Director. Despite a wide age gap, or perhaps because of it and their common Welsh ancestry, a warm relationship developed between the two men. One day a friend took them on a tour of the famous Osaka Castle. Afterwards, while the spell of the ancient beauty of the castle still held them, they were chatting quietly when Oswald said wistfully, 'But there's no one to write to; there's no one to share it with!'

Michael Griffiths has given another glimpse from those days. Oswald was speaking on the Prodigal Son when he dwelt on the sadness of the empty place at the table after the younger son had left. Then he opened his heart to his hearers as he spoke of the sorrow, the pain, that comes with the experience of the empty place at the table; such heartache as makes it impossible to eat.

He was lonely.

---

[1] Dr Michael C Griffiths MA, now Principal of the London Bible College.

12

Writer and Speaker

Very soon after Oswald had become General Director of the Mission, the other residents at 2 Cluny Road, Singapore, began to comment on the fact that anyone who was stirring at about 4 am, sometimes even earlier, would be likely to see a light in the General Director's study. Maybe they might see him making his morning cup of coffee. The morning hours, when the house was quiet, his mind fresh and clear, and he was safe from interruptions, had for many years been set apart not only for his regular devotions, but also for the preparation of messages and for writing. From his pen flowed a constant stream of articles for the OMF family and for a growing readership throughout the world. And it was during those morning hours that he wrote the books which were fast finding places on the shelves of Christians in many countries. By the time he had assumed the role of General Director, there were already six or seven titles bearing his name, and the number continued to increase.

But Oswald was far from satisfied with his performance as a writer, and Edith's letters to the family circle give an intimate picture of him restlessly striding about the room bemoaning his lack of style. She had responded with true homespun philosophy that since an increasing number of people were wanting to read his books, his style of writing did not seem to matter too much! Not that her reply satisfied him then, and he remains dissatisfied.

But while some may describe it as something of a bare-bones style ('I'm no good at padding,' he declares), yet those bones are strong bones. They are formed not only from an excellent vocabulary culled from his wide reading ('Never pass a word you don't know,' is a maxim learned from Joseph Kemp), but also from that fine feeling for words inherited from his father. The result is a style that is forceful, clear and easy to read. It is a style which is at its best when he is less concerned with the *abc* of teaching, than with inspiring, challenging and encouraging, as in such books as *Men From God's School*, *A Spiritual Clinic*, or *Towards Christian Maturity*; or in articles dealing with current world trends in missions. At such times he can carry the reader along with the momentum of his own eager thought.

Moreover, what Oswald has to say is the fruit of years of careful study and deep thought, resulting in such a thorough assimilation of the material with which he is concerned that it flows fresh and vibrant from his pen. He has under God's hand achieved what years ago he set out to do – to translate the deep things of God into language that all may understand.

J O Sanders is not a theologian, nor is he concerned to teach the theology of the cloister or the study. Rather does he seek to lead the average reader to an understanding of the ultimate basic truths of theology, and of their relevance to life in the context of the place where he lives and works; in the home, the workshop; on the farm; in the laboratory or the classroom; or in the world of business.

Yet writing has never been easy for him, and he writes not so much because he wants to as because he *must*. He sees writing as a God-given tool that surrendered back to Him becomes an instrument for the Holy Spirit's use. Getting started on a new book is always the hardest part – that stirring up of the mind to grapple with the subject. Then there is the careful selection of all relevant material from his extensive files. This he lists on wide-margined pages. Next he who hates detail must annotate each entry with meticulous care and begin assembling it under various headings. Starting to rough it out follows and only after the spade work has been done does the writing take over and begin to grow apace so that he *must* finish it. By that time it has all been written out three times – in longhand. He 'cannot think on the typewriter'. Always he must think with a pen in his hand. It may be a carry-over from his days in the law firm when almost everything had then to be written by hand. Doubtless, too, his clear, even handwriting was formed then. And it is still clear and even in his eighties, in spite of the loss of the top joint of his index finger in an accident with a lawn mower. Regardless of pain and discomfort he just went ahead and learned to write without his forefinger!

Before her final illness Edith had always typed his manuscripts, but for a good many years now his niece, Mrs Peggy Adair, has performed this task. His own part will not be finished until he has read the final proofs. All this work would be demanding enough if he could do it in the ordered quiet of his own study, but much of it must continue while he is 'on the road'.

Today J Oswald Sanders is known more as a writer than as a speaker because his books reach places where he is never likely to go. So a girl not long converted from the drug scene excitedly tells her friends of a wonderful book she has discovered in a small-town Christian book-shop. Its title was *A Spiritual Clinic*[1] and it had first been

---

[1] Also published under the title: *Problems of Christian Discipleship*

published nearly thirty years earlier. It was based on addresses Oswald had given at conferences and missionary retreats the world over, and he had thought rather poorly of it when he submitted it for publication. But it amazed everyone by proving a best seller and has been published in several languages. And still it goes on answering people's problems!

Another book, *The Incomparable Christ*[1], was first published in 1952. More than thirty years later a library assistant, a devout Roman Catholic, was browsing in a Catholic bookshop when the title arrested her. She had never heard of the author but she bought the book which has become a rich source of inspiration during her meditations on the person and work of Christ. Because of its subject matter, Oswald enjoyed writing this book more than any other, but he considers *Spiritual Leadership* to be his best work. It represents the distillation of two series of addresses given at successive sessions of council, and prepared for publication at the urgent request of the men to whom they were first addressed. Now it has become required reading for a number of Bible colleges and seminaries. Many pastors require their church officers to read it.

It is obvious that much of what Oswald has written has been based on lectures and addresses given over a long, active career. But those who have been able to hear him speak have enjoyed an added dimension. Undoubtedly it has to do with that mysterious God-given ability to project himself into the minds and hearts of an audience. It is a gift that can so rivet the attention of the average audience of all ages that even a fifty-minute address does not seem long, and a hard seat seems softer!

There are no flamboyant gestures; no impassioned appeals to the emotions. He just stands there, seeming

---

[1] First published as: *Christ Incomparable*

quite relaxed, and talks to his hearers. It is the voice that holds them. Strong, clear, well-modulated and well-measured, it is easy to listen to, easy to follow. Most of all it is the eyes that reveal the intensity behind the quiet manner. Even in quite a large auditorium a listener may feel those eyes searching him out, as though the speaker is addressing *him*, *his* problem, *his* sin. Oswald says frankly that he always 'goes for a verdict' whenever he speaks. Certainly there are always those who respond at some level of Christian experience. This is not to imply that he frequently makes appeals; he does not. He seeks rather to win a deep response from the hearts and minds of listeners. A few will speak to him after a meeting. From others he may hear years later of how much they were helped at a certain meeting.

Of necessity he repeats some addresses over the years, the most notable being his now-famous sermon on Caleb. He has lost count of the number of times he has preached on Caleb, and the universal appeal of the subject ensures its continued use. But in an average year of almost constant speaking tours perhaps up to a third of his addresses will have been specially prepared for particular occasions.

As a convention speaker he has always been especially appreciated as one who seeks neither to impress nor to entertain. Two of Oswald's close associates, who have had long links with the Keswick movement, talked recently of him as a convention speaker and were remarkably close in their assessments of him. They were speaking independently on different occasions and both men went straight to the point of the simplicity of Oswald's preaching that stems from a wide knowledge of Scripture but never seeks to impress; never makes his hearers feel small. This simplicity is a part of his logicality and his ability to translate tremendous truths into very simple propositions that can add up to an exceptionally clear statement of Keswick teaching.

Both men spoke of the aptness of the illustrations drawn from his wide reading, Ralph Davis adding that if sometimes his illustrations might appear to be over-simplistic, they had the great virtue of making the point and *only* the point.

Oswald Sanders uses a minimum of nervous energy when he is preaching. While this may be wrongly con-strued as coldness, Leonard Buck sees it for what it really is – a quite deliberate playing down of his own person-ality lest it impinge upon the work of the Holy Spirit in exalting Christ. Whether as speaker or writer, that is Oswald Sanders' ultimate aim – that in all things Christ may have the supremacy.

13

A Leap of Faith

Towards the end of 1966 Oswald realised that the search
for a man to replace himself as General Director had
become a matter of priority. He has always held strongly
to the view that no one should continue in office beyond
the agreed term. The end of that term was the time to
step out and make way for a younger successor. He had
already agreed reluctantly to an extension of two years
simply because no successor had yet emerged. But now
he was determined that there should be no further
extension. So in faith he drew up a list of the qualifications he should look for in the one whose name he would
submit to the Mission directors for consideration. It was
certainly a daunting list and in retrospect he laughingly
acknowledged that he had not complied with his own
requirements!

In spite of the Fellowship's generous acceptance of his
complete lack of field experience, he sensed that now the
mood was for a man from the field: one who had come up
through the ranks and had personally experienced their
special problems. The crisis of the post-China era was
long past and the Mission was firmly on course in the
new fields. So that was where he must begin his search
for a man who above all else must give evidence of a
depth of spiritual maturity. This would be reflected in

the quality of his field ministry and in his relationships with his fellow missionaries and their personal problems. If he measured up in those areas then he would surely be acceptable to all on the fields, especially if he had already proved himself in some area of leadership. Finally, he must be a good communicator, both on the platform and as a writer. These last two qualifications would certainly be essential not only in areas of field leadership but even more in relation to the Christian public in all the home countries.

As he prayed and pondered over the matter, Oswald found himself drawn back again and again to the name of one man. He had not seen a great deal of him, but he had talked with him at some length and had carefully followed his record.

Michael Griffiths and his wife Valerie both held Masters degrees from Cambridge and Oxford Universities respectively, and had arrived on the Japan field from England in 1958. Before applying to the OMF, Michael Griffiths had served acceptably on the staff of the IVF and had been active in promoting the cause of foreign missions among students. Furthermore he had proved himself as a writer with the wide and enthusiastic acceptance of his books, *Take My Life* and *Consistent Christianity*. Yes, his was certainly a name to be considered.

But Oswald knew he must be very sure before he made a move. So prayer and quiet investigations continued, while at the same time he remained open to any thoughts or suggestions concerning others who might be considered. But other names seemed to rule themselves out almost as soon as considered. He began to share his thinking with Arnold Lea and other directors, and prayer was intensified as together they sought guidance from God. There was so much at stake; they must be sure as to whether or not they should approach this young man.

Meanwhile although the conviction grew in Oswald's mind that this was God's answer to their seeking, none was more conscious than he that it would involve a bold leap of faith. Michael Griffiths had at the time served only nine years on the field and was not much known in the Fellowship beyond the Japan field. It would mean asking a great deal of the membership to respond positively to such a proposal, even remembering that it would be a further two years before he would assume office. It was true that D E Hoste, whom Hudson Taylor had appointed as his successor, and who became a legend within the Mission in his own life time, was only a year or so older than Michael Griffiths would be at the time of taking office. But Hoste had been known from the outset as a member of the famous 'Cambridge Seven', and later for his outstanding service during sixteen years in China. Nevertheless it did now appear as though God was directing Oswald towards this bold step of faith.

So believing that God would confirm His leading to the man of His choice, Michael Griffiths was invited to Singapore for discussions. Not surprisingly he was utterly confounded when Oswald put the suggestion to him, but he was willing to think and pray about it. Back in Japan he and his wife together faced the implications for them and their family if they were to take what for them, too, would indeed be a leap of faith. It would involve a complete shift in direction in their service: perhaps even more for the wife than for her husband. They must be sure that God was pointing the way. So when they had reached that point of assurance, and Oswald was at last free to bring forward the name of Michael Griffiths for consideration by all full members, God had already indicated His will at three different levels. Oswald's letter to members of the Fellowship, inviting comments and reactions, produced the expected ripples of astonishment but they soon subsided as, with few exceptions, the whole Fellowship acknowledged the evidence of God's leading. Michael Griffiths was accepted as the new General Director designate.

Looking back from the perspective of later years, Oswald's initiative in this matter can be seen as one of the most significant of those taken during his period of leadership. Right then it meant for him that once again he must reluctantly consent to a further extension of his term of office. Remembering his own early 'sink or swim' experience, he readily agreed that his young successor should have a period of twelve months to enable him to get the feel of things and find his feet at International Headquarters.

14

New Beginnings

Meanwhile, along with the search for his successor, Oswald had been continuing his busy schedule in different quarters of the globe. Towards the latter part of 1967 he was in London when he heard that an old friend of his and Edith's from New Zealand was also in London and he arranged to meet her at New Zealand House.

Mary Miller was the daughter of Oswald's old boss, Joseph Kemp, so their acquaintance stretched back over a long period. She had been a member of that memorable Beach Mission team when he and Edith had acted as 'house parents' on their honeymoon! After Mary's marriage to Rev John P Miller the two couples had maintained fairly close contact during their New Zealand days, and now Mary had been a widow for several years.

Time passed quickly as they talked over past days and caught up on family news while they shared afternoon tea. For Oswald the meeting was nothing more than a brief stop at a pleasant oasis in that desert of loneliness through which he had been travelling since Edith's death. But for Mary Miller it was much more. She too was desperately lonely and she saw the meeting as a pin-point of light at the end of a dark tunnel. And she seemed to see that light growing until its radiance should embrace them both. Much later she told Oswald that

God had given her the assurance that this would be so.

But Oswald was completely absorbed in the affairs that more than filled his days and it was some months before he thought much about Mary Miller. Then he began to consider how much they had in common: the years of shared memories and the mutual regard and respect for one another; surely these formed a good basis on which to build a closer relationship. Could this be what lay beyond the door that Edith had so generously opened for him? Well, he could at least write to her. Mary welcomed his letter, and the correspondence continued.

Towards the middle of 1968 Oswald was in India for a series of meetings at the invitation of Rev Ian Kemp, Mary's nephew, with whose family he was staying. Ian Kemp has recalled not only the great appreciation of Oswald's ministry to national workers and Western Missionaries alike at their summer retreats, but also his family's enjoyment of Oswald's genial company on their outings and picnics. He was the perfect guest and he was fun to be with, yet there was always a ready ear to listen to problems. But there was something else that Ian Kemp only learned later, and with great surprise.

Whether or not that relaxed family atmosphere acted as the final catalyst, it was while staying with the Kemps that Oswald wrote his proposal of marriage to Mary Miller. She needed no time to make up her mind and so after Oswald had informed the OMF directors of his intentions, the engagement was announced in July and they were married in Auckland in the following September, amid great rejoicing among both families.

Mary had very little knowledge of the Mission that absorbed most of Oswald's time, so it had been a big thing to ask her to spend that first year of marriage moving around with him among hundreds of people who were total strangers to her, but she was quite undaunted. She had so much to bring to that marriage: possessed of an outgoing personality, she was punctilious in her own way, and competent in all she did. As a well-trained musician she was an accomplished pianist with a good singing voice. And during her years as the wife of a Baptist pastor these gifts had been used and developed, while her courage and her strong faith had sustained her during a life which had known its full share of difficulty and sorrow. These experiences had not, however, in any way dulled her sense of fun. She was an excellent companion and together she and Oswald soon developed a richly satisfying relationship.

Such support eased greatly for Oswald the pressures of that last demanding year in office. She was even able to use her stenographic skills to help him with his work.

Six months of that year were spent in North America and it was while they were in California that Oswald wrote his last General Director's letter to the members of the beloved OMF family, that was published in their *Bulletin* of October 1969. It was longer than usual; there was so much on his heart, and especially what he knew would be the needs of the new General Director:

For my successor, Michael Griffiths, to whom I most gladly pass on the torch on October 1, I can ask nothing more than that you be as generous and gracious to him as you have been to me . . . That he will make mistakes as I have done is likely since he is human, but they will probably be fewer. His age, his training, his experience and his spiritual stature qualify him for leadership in the complex and demanding world of today. Incidentally, I was interested to read the dictum of a great leader some time ago . . . 'Never appoint to a top position a man whom you can count on never to make a mistake!' Such a man would be so cautious, he would never give strong and daring leadership . . .

Have you ever thought that the time a leader needs your

loyalty most is when things are difficult and you question his judgement . . . ? I am not pleading for an uncritical acceptance of decisions made, but for loyalty even though you feel there has been an error of judgement. This means more than you think.

Then later there followed a gracious look back: 'I wish to record what a joy and privilege it has been to work with Arnold Lea in a very close and harmonious partnership . . . I say what I know to be true, that the heaviest burdens of leadership have rested on him, although this may not have always been apparent. Our debt as a fellowship to him is great indeed.'

And finally: '. . . the graciousness and faithfulness of a forbearing Lord . . . has exceeded all my expectations . . . "There hath not failed one word of all His good promise."'

In September Oswald and Mary returned to Singapore and Oswald began the task of handing over office. At the final farewell Arnold Lea's tribute came from the heart as he spoke of Oswald's 'genuine unobtrusiveness':

He does not overwhelm you . . . He treats you as a human being meeting another human being – not with an impressive display of gifts or learning . . . Perhaps his greatest contribution has been to encourage us all to do more than we thought we could do, as he challenged us to the highest. And yet with true humility he will accept from a committee advice which may be contrary to the way he is thinking . . .

The messages that remain in my memory are those which have been studies of individuals: Elijah . . . Jacob . . . Joshua . . . Paul . . . These have been insights into human nature and its weakness, with man's response to God's provision of strength. This understanding of human nature has been the very characteristic which has made his leadership so outstanding.

Then, in lighter vein, after commenting on the amount of work Oswald got through in the early morning hours while most people were asleep: 'It was not surprising that he had to make up for his lack of sleep somehow. On occasions it has been comforting to see the mighty, tireless J O S dozing in a committee meeting or even at Overseas Council!'

For Oswald, what must have been the natural regret of stepping down from the leadership of such a close, warm fellowship, was eased by the invitation of the Directorate to become a Consulting Director of the OMF. In his mid-eighties he continues to be valued in this capacity.

It must be admitted that retirement brought also a very human sense of release. Friends still recall how he thrust back his shoulders as though he were shrugging off a physical burden and smiling broadly he breathed: 'No more committees! No more decisions about other people's lives!'

Not that Oswald saw his retirement as being in any way the end of the line. He had just stepped out of the most demanding role of his career, grateful for the limitless grace and strength that had been adequate for every demand of those fifteen years. Now he was equally grateful that the time had come to exchange that role for a new, but less demanding one.

'Retirement is always a critical experience that appears to have about it an aura of finality,' he wrote in an issue of the OMF Bulletin in 1982. 'The process of aging is gradual, but retirement is not gradual. Yesterday I was on the active list, today I am on the retired list. I have no choice in the matter. Unless the mind has previously been conditioned, one is likely to feel significantly older the day after retirement. The important chapter of life is completed. But actually that is an illusion. The essential person is exactly the same. All that is changed is that we have been given a new assignment in a different venue.' And: 'Always have a little more than you can comfortably cope with,' is his inspiriting advice to those who are facing retirement.

For himself that 'little more' would include some lecturing at the Bible college in Auckland, as well as keeping up with a busy schedule of meetings, and, of course, writing. Making a garden around the home he and Mary planned to establish would provide exercise and relaxation. He is no mean gardener and for fifteen years he had to forego the pleasure of growing things that had been fostered during those holidays on his uncle's farm.

No doubt there were some regrets as he stood on the deck of the freighter, the *Thorsorient*, watching the skyline of Singapore recede from view. But the past, along with its mistakes, could safely be left with God. Right then Oswald's concern was with the future that held such bright promise. That, too, was safe in God's hands.

15
Not Offended

After he and Mary had settled back into life in Auckland, Oswald was soon enjoying the greater freedom and lack of heavy responsibility in his new assignments. A friend of the early days in New Zealand remarked how wonderful it was to have 'the old Ossie' visiting them again. He no longer had 'that black bag' that had absorbed so much of his attention even on social visits during the past years. Now he was once again 'his old, laughing, teasing self'. Certainly the process of shedding that inhibiting cocoon was being greatly speeded up. He was home and he could relax.

It must have been about the middle of their first year at home that Mary began to experience difficulty with one of her hands. It was evident that there was loss of muscle tone at the base of the thumb. Alarm bells began to ring. A doctor recommended an operation but it did not help the condition. The diagnosis had to be faced – it was lateral sclerosis. The prognosis indicated a slow and irremedial loss of motive power.

Oswald was appalled. But the fact had to be accepted. Characteristically, Mary mustered all her resources and set out to fight the insidious onslaught with faith and courage. Many years earlier, when her husband had been critically ill, Oswald and Edith had joined her in believing prayer for his recovery and they had seen God give healing against all medical expectations. Now she wanted to prove God's healing power at work in her own body. Her chief anxiety was that she might 'let the Lord down' by lack of faith. For his part, Oswald's faith was rooted firmly in the unfailing love and unerring sovereignty of God. That had been his stance during Edith's illness and it continued to be so now.

Mary determined to do all she could to keep herself actively involved in life. When they had been in California prior to Oswald's retirement, a friend had suggested that Mary might like to take up painting and gave her a set of water-colours and brushes. She had not found the medium to her liking and did not pursue it. Now she decided to see what she might be able to do with oils. Recently her daughter's mother-in-law, an artist, had died and all her painting materials had been given to Mary. She had no lessons but soon found that she enjoyed working with oils. Her 'subjects' had perforce to be pictures that appealed to her, of which she made copies. From the first her paintings showed distinct ability and after she had produced about ten pictures she was urged to apply for membership of the New Zealand Fellowship of Artists. She submitted two paintings and was accepted right away. This boost to her morale encouraged her to continue painting after she could do little else. When the two fingers she used for painting failed, she contrived to use the other two. Altogether she produced about fifty pictures of remarkable quality. Some she sold, others she gave away and a few still hang in Oswald's home.

Meanwhile Oswald had heard of a hospital in Germany, in the Black Forest, that was having some success in their treatment of the disease, and determined to take Mary there.

At first there was definite and very encouraging improvement. For the first time for a long while she was able to go for a walk: as much as three quarters of a mile in the Black Forest. She had meals in the hospital dining room and Oswald was able to join her for dinner in the evenings when they shared a table with two German ladies who knew no English and they knew no German. Nonetheless, with the aid of an English-German dictionary they contrived to inject such a sparkling element of fun into these occasions as made them thoroughly enjoyable.

This element of fun and good humour continued to brighten even the difficult days. And there were many difficult days to follow. The promise of continued improvement that seemed to have been held out in Germany began to fade not long after their return home. Oswald had bought one of the machines used in the treatment, but Mary could not use it for long.

She continued to paint for as long as she could hold a brush, but the last picture was left only half finished. Surprisingly, the last skill she surrendered was that of driving the car. A competent driver for most of her life, she was sure she would know when she could no longer handle the car. It preserved for her a shred of independence. But there came the day when she shook her head when Oswald offered her the wheel. She knew the time had come.

The steady decline continued. Speech failed her during the last three months. She still managed to communicate a little by writing. Then that, too, went and Oswald had to watch her slowly slipping out of life in spite of all he could do. Faith must have been tried almost to the limit.

Was he ever tempted to ask *why*? That question *had* to be asked of him because it was so important to know his answer.

'No.' The answer came quietly and with deep assurance. He had learned that lesson from his sister when he had accompanied her to the hospital where her husband was dying. In a definite act of committal the young wife had given her loved one back to God, ending with the words, 'And in the years to come I will never ask you *why*?' He had never forgotten that prayer and he knew she had never questioned God's ways, even in the difficult years that followed. Now, although like the imprisoned John the Baptist he might not understand the ways of his Lord, and might even be baffled by those ways, yet he was 'not offended'.

Mary slipped out of the shadows into the radiance of God's presence on 10 December, 1972. Her nephew, Rev Ian Kemp, gives a glimpse of that time:

> When I returned to New Zealand in 1969 to be pastor of the Auckland Baptist Tabernacle, J O and Mary were members, so I now stood in a pastoral relationship to them both. When Mary died I conducted the funeral service in the Tabernacle, and was impressed with the quiet confidence with which he laid her to rest, this the second wife who had been taken from him after a long period of illness. His faith and his devotion to her, to the Lord, and to the truths of the Christian faith, were exemplary throughout. It was the same confidence which had impressed me when J O conducted the funeral of his own brother . . . a year or two earlier.

That was what his friends saw. His dignified bearing gave no hint of the appalling sense of loss within him: the devastation, desolation and the darkness – black darkness as in a tunnel that has no end, no light. But God was there:

> Let him who walks in the dark,
> who has no light,

trust in the name of the Lord
and rely on his God.
                    (Isaiah 50:10 NIV)

Even though I walk
through the darkest
  valley
I will fear no evil
for you are with me
(Psalm 23:4, NIV margin)

16

This Mountain

Across the Tasman, in the city of Melbourne, two men were deep in discussion. A crisis was facing the council administering the affairs of the Christian Leaders' Training College (CLTC) in Papua New Guinea, part of the large island immediately to the north of Australia. 'I believe Oswald Sanders is the man for the job.' The speaker was Mr Leonard Buck, Chairman of the council. 'We can't ask him; he has only just lost his wife,' protested the secretary.

The problem facing them concerned the appointment of a new Principal for the college. It was already mid-December and the school year would commence in February. They were looking for a man of wide experience and sound administrative ability. Above all they needed a man of vision who could lead his colleagues into the challenge of the future, when Papua New Guinea would be granted independence.

Next morning Leonard Buck again spoke to the secretary: 'I am absolutely sure we should ask Oswald,' he said. Then he put through a call to Oswald's home in Auckland.

Oswald was well-informed about the affairs of the CLTC. He had been a member of the council of the Bible college in Melbourne when the idea of establishing a college for nationals in Papua New Guinea had first begun to take shape during the years immediately following the second world war. Since leaving Melbourne he had continued to follow developments and especially after the opening of the college in 1965. Nevertheless the proposal put to him by his friend came as a complete surprise. In his present state of mind he needed time to absorb it. All he could say was that he would pray about it. Yet even as he turned away from the telephone he believed he knew the answer. There was a gleam of light in the darkness.

In one of Edith's letters that had shared so much with the family at home, she had referred to the prodigious amount of time and effort Oswald put into preparing messages and in writing. 'I don't believe he could live without it,' she had written.

Now Oswald began to sense that this invitation was God's answer to his need. It was work that he loved: it would fill most of his days, and provide the change of scene and occupation that he sorely needed. Best of all it held a challenge that he was ready to meet. 'It saved my life,' he says in retrospect.

When it became known that in his seventy-first year Oswald was embarking on a project that would make such demands upon him, it was almost inevitable that he would be regarded as a modern Caleb. But it is doubtful whether such an idea would have occurred to him. Caleb was an old man of eighty-five when he asked Joshua for 'this mountain'. At seventy, the thought of growing old had never so much as crossed Oswald's mind! He did not *feel* old, nor did he *look* old, and any suggestion that he might be growing old would have been greeted by those expressive raised eyebrows!

Oswald's 'mountain' did not present any obvious 'missionary hardships'. The college which had a staff of thirty expatriates and twenty nationals, was situated in the highlands of Papua New Guinea where the climate was healthy and mild and very different from the steamy jungles of the lowlands. The area had been opened up to modern transport during the second world war, with a centre at Mt Hagen, not too many miles from the CLTC. Government requirements that all formal teaching should be in English, meant that Oswald did not have to cope with a language barrier. Special courses trained the students in ways of presenting spiritual truths in pidgin and the vernacular.

He was welcomed by the expatriate staff as a trusted leader whose vision and experience could lead them into the future, and as a father-figure to them and their families. He was double the age of the oldest staff member, and their children may well have regarded Oswald, with his gentle approach to little children, as a substitute grandfather.

He had been somewhat taken aback when he had first met the students, most of whom were little more than a step removed from the stone age. The wonder was that they should have advanced so far in so short a time. But he realised that he had not been prepared for them to be so different from the thousands of other students he had met in many countries. Although these Pacific Islanders might speak English, many still retained the thought patterns of their ancestors. He had been asked to teach the Book of Romans! Just how was he to convey abstract ideas to those who could only think in concrete terms? However, the warm-hearted students responded happily to what they soon perceived to be a genuine love and concern for them, even if some could not always follow his lectures!

> For me, 'twas not the truth you taught,
> To you so clear – to me so dim,

But when you came you brought to me –
A sense of Him.

Author unknown

Nevertheless it was also abundantly clear that as with students the world over, opportunity was a key factor in their progress. Those who had had the advantage of a good grounding in Western education at mission schools, and especially high schools, certainly had the edge over their less privileged companions. Some of the former could have held their own almost anywhere.

As he had surmised, the oversight of the busy programme absorbed his time all through the week. But the weekends were different. He dreaded the weekends. They were long and very lonely. He had time to think and time to remember. Mary and he had not been long together, but for the greater part of that time she had been such a cheerful, such a gallant companion. And it did not seem to grow any easier to fight back the loneliness that pressed upon his spirit. But God was there, the 'God [who] fills the place of all He takes away'. From all over Papua New Guinea came invitations to speak at special gatherings of missionaries. Beginning in May 1973 until nearly the end of the next year, planes of the Missionary Aviation Fellowship ferried Oswald over the rugged highlands to a succession of missionary conferences and retreats. From the Word of God and out of his own deep need he spoke to the needs of the men and women he met. Jaded spirits were renewed and they found fresh courage to face the problems, the discouragements and often the loneliness of their circumstances.

He made many new friends, and his own vision gained in perspective when from time to time he learned something of what the students would face when they returned home. The lonely weekends still had to be faced, but this added dimension to his life and work in Papua New Guinea, gave fresh impetus to all he did.

Initially he had agreed to go to the CLTC for six months, but that was soon changed to two years. By the second year Oswald was hoping that he might be able to hand over his responsibilities as Principal to a Papua New Guinean. The council had their eyes on a man who they hoped would be available by the end of 1975. In that case Oswald would have been willing to stay for a third year. But it was not to be, so he turned his attention to grooming a young expatriate staff member to take over at the end of 1974.

The approach of Independence made it very desirable that the control of the CLTC should be handed over to a locally-based council and this in turn would mean registration of the college under the laws of Papua New Guinea before Independence Day. Time was running out, and considering that legal transactions tended to drag on interminably, and that the nearest lawyer was 300 miles away, it seemed unlikely that registration could be achieved before the important day. But as Oswald turned the matter over in his mind, his memory began to stir. It was almost fifty years since he had practised law, but it was just possible that he might be able to prepare the necessary document. It was worth a try. Using such relevant material as he could lay his hands on, and with the help of his colleagues, he drew up the required Memorandum and Articles of Association which the Vice-Principal took down to the Registrar of Societies. Half expecting a rebuff, he was delighted to be able to carry back the good news that their application had been accepted. The CLTC was registered as a Papua New Guinean Institution before Independence Day.

The value of those two years of Oswald's contribution to the CLTC has been summed up by Leonard

Buck in his preface to the story of the early years of the college[1]:

> Mr J. Oswald Sanders was quite obviously God's man to guide in the localisation of the CLTC Council, and his two years as Principal – 1973 and 1974 – saw a great leap forward. It was during this time that the administrative base and responsibility moved from the Melbourne Bible Institute to a locally based and partly indigenous Council. The patience, grace, and firmness of Mr Sanders, Secretary to the new Council as well as Principal of the College, and with the wisdom born of his experience, greatly assisted in getting the College Council off to an effective start on its own.
>
> Another side product – or perhaps a main one in this period of the College growth, wisely promoted by Mr Sanders, was the accelerating administrative and spiritual maturity of the College Faculty, ensuring a smooth and most effective take-over of the Principalship by the then Dean, John Hitchen, in 1975.

---

[1] *Planting Men in Melanesia* J O Sanders

17

The Plough of the Lord

When Oswald returned to Auckland in November 1974 it was natural that he and his sister Mrs Rita Ford should make their home together. The brother-sister bond had been a very close one since childhood and Rita had been his strong support during the illnesses of first Edith and then Mary. She was still quite active although she must have been beginning to feel the limitations of advancing years. The eldest of her three children, Beryl, who had had to retire from missionary service in Eritrea after a severe attack of hepatitis, was in a nursing post in Auckland and so able to give help from time to time as needed.

Ever since the death of Rita's husband, Oswald had stood in a special relationship to her children. Beryl had never married and so, with her missionary vocation, it was not surprising that she was particularly close to Oswald. After his return from Papua New Guinea she suggested that he should get a home where the three of them could live, so that she would be able to look after him and her mother. It seemed to be an ideal plan, especially looking to future needs, and Oswald set about doing just that. He bought a house where Rita could live independently in one section and he and Beryl in the rest of the house, with special provision for Beryl's own private area where she could entertain young nurses for whom she had a deep concern and who responded to her friendly hospitality.

From January to the end of June Oswald had engagements in Australia, including an emergency stint for one term at the Bible college in Melbourne. By the time he could return to Auckland Beryl had finished all the preparations for their new home and the trio settled in happily. It was just ideal for all their needs.

One month later it was discovered that Beryl had developed cancer. She lived only three months longer.

Once again brother and sister walked that dark valley together. Although Oswald felt that he had to give his strength to comforting Rita, he too mourned deeply for Beryl as for a dearly-loved daughter.

'Why should I start at the plough of my Lord, that maketh deep furrows in my soul? I know He is no idle husbandman. He purposeth a crop,' wrote Samuel Rutherford. More than 300 years later Oswald echoed the thought of the rugged old Scot, when he talked of the succession of bereavements he had suffered:

I've no doubt that, looking back, those experiences were part of the price of the ministry. I think the Lord works something into you that doesn't come otherwise. I've always felt that it is not purposeless although it is not what you would choose. It's part of the unfolding of the plan. I know that something has been worked into me through those things, because I've had to work my way through and get on top each time. It affects you in your deepest parts but I've never been tempted to question the Lord on it because of the example my sister had set as a young widow.

Then he went on to refer to a letter written by Bishop Frank Houghton to Amy Carmichael of Dohnavur, India, after the death of his younger sister. 'It takes very high ground, but I agree with it,' he commented. Here is the passage to which he refers:

> Many of our friends, in their letters of sympathy, speak of God's mysterious ways, and I know there is an element of mystery. But I shrink from the suggestion that our Father has done anything that needs to be explained. What He has done is the best, because He has done it, and I pray that as a family we may not cast about for explanations, but exult in the Holy Spirit and say, 'I thank Thee, Father . . . Even so, Father . . .'
>
> It suggests a lack of confidence in Him if we find it necessary to understand all He does.
>
> Will it not bring greater joy to tell Him that we need no explanation because we know Him? 'As for God, his way is perfect,' said the psalmist. If His way is perfect, we need no explanations.[1]

Then, resuming his thought on what God had taught him through bereavement and other difficult experiences, Oswald continued:

> I know one thing it has done is to give me a line of ministry that has become more prominent latterly. I take the Disciplines that produce maturity: the Discipline of Disturbance; the Discipline of Darkness; the Discipline of Disappointment; the Discipline of Discrimination (the ways of the Lord are not equal) and the Discipline of Delay. All of these have been experiences I have known, and through which God has worked something into me that meets the need of other people. It is not something one is conscious of, but it works its way into the ministry without being conscious of it. It is *there*, and it *does* something.

Then he laughed as he recalled how prophetic had been the judgement of two matronly ladies as they

---

[1] Frank Houghton, *Amy Wilson Carmichael* (London SPCK, 1952).

discussed the preaching of the *very* young Oswald Sanders: 'He'll be all right after he's suffered!' Then he sobered again as he referred to an address he sometimes gives to ministers on *The Price of a Ministry*: 'All fruitfulness is touched with the Cross,' he said in conclusion.

18

Caleb

The death of Oswald's niece necessitated another move closer to Rita Ford's second daughter, Mrs Peggy Adair. In June 1976 he wrote to his friends: 'My sister who lives with me has to take things quietly, but we manage to make the grade quite well. I have the large garden I longed for and water it copiously with perspiration.'

That garden, for which he had to break the ground, was something of which any much younger man might have been proud – a delight to the eye and wonderfully productive. This taming of the landscape to conform to his own design satisfies some basic need as well as absorbing his energies. For her part, Rita Ford was delighted to be able to make a home for the younger brother of whom she was so deeply fond and immensely proud. At the same time she felt it to be a sister's duty to make sure his feet were kept firmly on the ground!

While he was in Papua New Guinea the Missionary Aviation Fellowship had invited Oswald to give the main addresses at their annual conference. Unbeknown to him, it was a crucial period for them and God had wonderfully used him to speak to their particular needs. In grateful recognition the MAF had conferred upon him their highest honour by making him an Honorary Captain of their flight. When he wrote and told Rita that he had at last got his wings, her response had been typical: 'How wonderful! Now you can pack them away with your halo!'

There must have been something like a revival of the lively camaraderie of the old days before Rita's marriage when they had supported one another through the sudden storms that burst around them in the home. Rita's puckish humour was a match for Oswald's quick wit but there were never any hidden barbs in their lively exchanges. Privileged guests in that home carried away an unforgettable impression of the unfailing affection and concern for one another that glowed steadily beneath the sparkle of their humour.

In another of his regular letters to his friends, Oswald referred to 'my sister . . . who shares in my work'. That 'sharing' referred to her constant and detailed prayer support which never wavered over the years. It is interesting, too, to learn how Oswald encouraged her in prayer for an ever-widening group of people including a number of missionaries whom she came to know during these years. She had been inclined to think of herself as being of little account. This active participation in the lives of others through letters and prayer-involvement gave her a sense of sharing in the work of people whom she rarely if ever met. It became such a vital ministry that she was greatly valued by many in far-flung places who so appreciated the warm concern of her letters and the power of her prayers.

But none appreciated that support more than her brother. She was one of a number of friends who prayed daily for him. Again and again he speaks of the value of such prayer, urging others to cherish and cultivate all such commitments as being of greater value than pure gold.

Rita made no demur when increasing invitations made greater and greater demands upon Oswald's time so that she was without his company for longer and longer periods. Her daughter took care to see that she had all the help she needed, but inevitably by January 1980 he wrote: '. . . I am trying to sell my home as my nephew and niece and my sister (with whom I live) and I are planning to build two home units so that my sister can be closer to her daughter while I am away.' By the end of that year the move for both families had been completed and he could write: 'My sister and I are in our lovely new home . . . We have a magnificent view of Manukau Harbour and the Waitakere Ranges. Another garden to break in from scratch! God is good to us.'

There are some people to whom a view is of paramount importance when choosing a site for a home and Oswald is one of them. For the gospel's sake he will live cheerfully in any corner, but when he is free to choose he will always seek a space where he can look into the distance, or at least on an outlook that can lift his sights and his mind beyond the immediate environs. This particular block had hung fire on the market because of seemingly insurmountable difficulties in developing it. Now these had been overcome and they were able to enjoy the superb views. If anything could have held him at home surely that view and the exciting prospect of the new garden might have done so. But there were so many opportunities that called for the exercise of his special gifts, and they pulled with greater appeal than the most comfortable home or the most magnificent vista. An old mystic once wrote: 'Gently loosens He thine hold of the treasured former things . . . and alone, alone He stands reaching forth beseeching hands.' Nearly fifty years had passed since the young Oswald Sanders had set his sights on the way of the Cross and that still held his vision clear above all lesser things.

'It isn't that I have itchy feet,' he wrote to his friends, 'but when the Lord opens so many doors of service, I feel that I must enter them while I have the strength to do so. I am very conscious that continuing health and ability to minister is a fragile gift of God and greatly value the prayers of friends who share the ministry.'

It meant, too, that he must forego much of the pleasure of making that garden. His increasing absences meant that it was natural that his nephew should care for it. Not that he relinquished all interest in it, and still delights to be able to work off his energies in it.

Earlier that year, on 13 June 1980, Oswald had received a telegram from the Governor General of New Zealand. It read:

I HAVE MUCH PLEASURE IN INFORMING YOU THAT THE QUEEN HAS BEEN GRACIOUSLY PLEASED ON THE OCCASION OF HER MAJESTY'S BIRTHDAY TO CONFER UPON YOU THE HONOUR OF OFFICER OF THE CIVIL DIVISION OF THE MOST EXCELLENT ORDER OF THE BRITISH EMPIRE STOP PLEASE ACCEPT MY WARM CONGRATULATIONS STOP OFFICIAL ANNOUNCEMENT WILL BE MADE TOMORROW MORNING
KEITH HOLYOAKE
GOVERNOR GENERAL

Oswald never learned who had been responsible for putting his name forward in recognition of his work with the Bible college of New Zealand. Of course he disclaims any worthiness on his part, but he was glad that such recognition should be made of the value of a spiritual work within the nation.

Some may be surprised that during a life of worldwide public ministry Oswald Sanders has received no honorary degrees. At the end of his service at the Bible college of New Zealand it was suggested that he should allow his name to be submitted for ordination in the Baptist church. He declined for no other reason than that he had not earned it! He was not academically qualified. Later, during his years as OMF General Director, he was offered an honorary doctorate by a Christian University in the USA. Again he declined on the grounds of lacking academic qualifications.

'They were hurt,' he said, 'but I felt I had not earned it. I don't know whether it would have been better for OMF if I had accepted it. But it did not seem to be right for me. I had no academic qualifications. I'm quite happy to be plain "Mr".'

The following year Rita suffered a series of strokes and passed away on 21 November 1981, exactly six years after the death of her daughter Beryl. Oswald had cut short an overseas tour and was able to be with her at the last. While it is true that her death in her eighties did not have the same poignancy as the other griefs he had suffered, he did feel her loss very keenly. Theirs had been such a close relationship since childhood and in recent years she had been his closest companion and support. The spectre of loneliness could again have reared its ugly head. That it did not overwhelm him, though undoubtedly present, has been due in very great measure to the love and concern of his nephew and niece, Robin and Peggy Adair. Oswald still maintains his own home, but most evenings when he is at home he enjoys dinner with them, followed by a game of Scrabble with Peggy while Robin makes his contribution by washing up! This helps to satisfy his need of family closeness. Mary's daughter, Barbara, is always welcoming. He would like to see more of his grandchildren, but Cambridge, England, is a long way away and the times when he can avail himself of the welcome that always awaits him in Wilbur's home are all too rare.

Happy memories of his early friendship with George Ford are revived when Oswald is able to visit Rita's son in Australia. In spite of more than one debilitating illness, Gerald Ford still retains much of the ebullient sense of humour that had characterised his father. And there could be few more heart-warming pictures than the sight of the tall, broad-framed, smiling 'J O' walking hand in hand with a very small great-great-niece (Gerald's grand-daughter) trotting contentedly by his side.

Family household moves often have a way of bringing to light old treasures, and a recent move in Oswald's family uncovered one such small treasure. It is a bundle of letters that he had written to his sister and family during overseas tours in 1979–81. Nowhere do we get such a clear picture of the warm family man as in these hastily-penned missives, that appear to have been weekly bulletins. The postmarks tell their own story of the pressures of constant travel in England, Wales and Scotland; in Switzerland and Germany; in the USA and Canada; and back through Singapore and Papua New Guinea. They were dashed off in odd moments while waiting for transport to meetings, or at air terminals and occasionally in flight. Edith used to complain that he never gave enough detail. These letters are full of detail: of his doings, of people he meets, and of places he enjoys. There is even the occasional echo of Edith's 'If only you could enjoy it too!' In every letter there is eager comment on family news received, or very evident disappointment when he has found no letter awaiting him on arrival at successive destinations, or delight when a batch of mail catches up with him.

Most revealing of all is the signature at the bottom of every letter. It is simply, *Ossie*. Very early in his life, at the outset of his growing public ministry, a wise friend had advised Oswald to discourage the use of the homely diminutive that had been part of his boyhood. He pointed out that it did not accord well with the image of leadership. The use of the initial of his first name, *John*, combined with his full second name would provide an admirable by-line for his writings. Increasingly, the name of *J Oswald Sanders* became a familiar one in New Zealand and abroad. When he moved across to Australia, the old name was left behind. Edith had never used it. During his years as General Director of CIM-OMF, colleagues became very familiar with the signature *Oswald* at the conclusion of many hundreds of letters, and it has been the signature on his prayer-letters to friends the world over. But in these intimate family communications the old name, belonging to the days when he was the youngest in the family, came most naturally. That he had long been its acknowledged head did not weigh with him at all; he is quite without pretension. When Dr Paul White was speaking of his experience of 'J O' as a completely natural person, 'always available, always approachable', he had added the remark: 'When you've got great people they're either pompous or they're unconscious of their status.'

The 'Caleb' years have not been all work; there has been time to relax in a way he has seldom done before. Having lived in Melbourne for eight years (1946–54), it was impossible for him not to have been infected by the seasonal excitement of the Victorian Football League competitions – Australian Rules variety; all the more so because he had lived in the heart-land of the 'Mighty Hawks'. However, it is doubtful whether he would have allowed himself to watch a match. Nowadays, not only does he follow with interest the fortunes of New Zealand's own All Blacks, but he maintains a keen interest in the VFL competitions in Melbourne. Leonard Buck recalls an afternoon in recent years when he and Oswald enjoyed watching a game at the Melbourne Cricket Ground, and especially the latter's spontaneous enjoyment of an amusing incident. They found themselves among a group of high spirited young people who were imbibing rather freely. At a point in the game when feelings were running high a young fellow began excitedly waving his can of beer high in the air, spilling the contents over Leonard Buck's head. Oswald roared with laughter: 'Well, I've seen some odd baptisms,' he said, 'but never one with a can of beer!'

One of the most amazing aspects of these years is his continuing appeal to young people. He has been *Uncle Oswald* to at least one group of overseas students. It seems that when young people are concerned to give priority to discovering God's highest purposes for them they find reality and clarity in Oswald's uncompromising standards of discipleship.

Undoubtedly his appeal stems from a genuine interest in the concerns of the young people he meets, as instanced in this paragraph from a letter:

To me it is significant to see how our family reacts to the frequent guests who stay at our home. Young people particularly are able to spot a phony and there have been a few phonies . . . from time to time! But Mr Sanders certainly doesn't fall into that category by their standards. In fact our boys have remarked several times how much they have enjoyed and appreciated him because of the personal interest he has taken in them and not just in the adults in the home . . . One time we were getting ready [for] a holiday that would take in a day at Disney World. After he left our home we discovered an envelope in the guest-room containing a thank-you note along with a money gift for the boys to have a good time at Disney World. To me that personal touch is the mark of a warm, sensitive man of God and not just an austere, unapproachable missionary statesman.

And this from another letter:

Our seventeen-year-old daughter was not at home when he arrived. She was learning to be a cashier in a grocery store, and was trying to learn all the many codes. As she came in, Mr Sanders asked for the sheet and began testing her! As it was winter-time and the ground often slippery, Jeanette took it upon herself to help Mr Sanders in and out of the church and one day he said, 'My grand-daughter is helping me,' and from then on he was Grandpa Sanders to her.

A young home-staff worker had been detailed to drive J O to a morning appointment. She had had a difficult weekend and while she coped with the frustrations of the morning traffic, her reactions to the problems she had been experiencing began to spill over from time to time. Oswald sat quietly, making little comment.

She had been told that he would certainly be asked to remain for lunch at the end of the morning, so that she was taken aback to hear him courteously decline the invitation to lunch. She concluded that 'the dear old gentleman was tired out, of course' and prepared to get him back as soon as possible.

They were no sooner on their way than he surprised her again by asking briskly, 'Where can we find a place to eat?'

'He bought me a lovely lunch and while we ate he got me talking.' It was a relief just to talk to a sympathetic listener who understood her problems so well. As she talked she began to see it all in perspective so that she was ready to absorb the spiritual counsel he finally offered her.

Older people who have heard Oswald speak many times over the years all insist that he is 'better than ever'. They find an added depth that evokes deeper responses in their own hearts, and always there is the freshness of a mind and heart that draws its life continually from the living spring.

One letter that has come out of these 'Caleb' years is worth quoting at length:

He has often stayed here, sometimes for weeks, always to our great enjoyment and blessing. I cannot remember a cross word from him.

We never knew him to miss or be late for an appointment. If we set times for meals or pickup to a meeting, he was always ready to go on time. Heavy as his schedule is there never seems to be a sense of hurry in meeting it.

Oswald's life is most consistent. One does not find him preaching consideration to others and then practising impatience in the privacy of the home . . . For some years we entertained renowned Christian leaders and speakers. Often we were sadly disappointed in the selfishness, petulance or self-indulgence of some while out of the public eye. This was never noticeable in Oswald.

He loves New Zealand and his own home there – so often talking about his view, his garden, his neighbours and loved ones. I think he had, but hid, deep, deep feelings over loss of the nearest members of his household.

The busy round of meetings left little time for evenings of recreation. However, Oswald loves a game of Scrabble – and is very good at it. Sometimes he comes out with esoteric or abstruse words, but the dictionary backs him up! He loves to be proved right.

It is hard to find warts . . . and I am not covering up known undesirable faults. He is a large man with a strong bodily presence. He is prominent in both appearance and status. Probably this keeps some people at bay – they feel him rather austere and his very quietness might make them think him 'colder' than some would a 'gusty' person.

In his mid-eighties Oswald Sanders is as alert and forward-looking as he was a quarter of a century earlier when he led the OMF into its second century with the forging of the New Instrument. In November 1987 he was able to write to his friends:

I have often preached on Caleb, one of my favourite characters, but never dreamed I would pass the age when he said to Joshua, 'Give me this mountain,' but now that point has been safely negotiated. At the time of my 85th birthday I was guest speaker at the Moody Bible Institute Missions Conference. Imagine my amazement when I went into the 1,000-seat dining room, to see a birthday cake, beautifully decorated, *seventeen feet long*! . . .

The highlight of the tour was [this] Moody Bible Institute Missions Conference in Chicago, at which I was entrusted with the six main messages . . . There were 1,450 students and 90 missionaries participating. The theme was The Crisis of the Crucial, and I believe the Lord helped me to deal with some crucial issues . . .

It was my intention to cut down the programme in 1988 somewhat, [He has been saying that for about six years!] but it hasn't worked out that way . . . 1988 is the Centenary of CIM-OMF in USA and Canada, and I have been booked for three months in Spring and three months in Autumn.

In between there will be conferences in Hong Kong, Singapore and Japan!

It is not that he goes looking for openings. Most open up naturally around OMF engagements. A few come looking for him. He has spoken several times at Navigator International Conferences. At one time when they were planning a conference that was to be concerned with the restructuring of administration, the leaders decided that they needed Oswald's presence and advice. They would pay his return air fare from New Zealand. He protested that surely it would not be worth the cost, but at their insistence he went. As he sat in on their discussions he was able to draw upon his wide experience in OMF to make a vital contribution that helped set the pattern for the future. It was a contribution, maintained their leader, that was worth many times the cost involved.

One leader had become over-busy to the point of collapse. He confided to Oswald that he was considering handing over his executive responsibilities to another to free himself for greater involvement in the overall spiritual leadership. What would Oswald advise? 'Do it!' responded Oswald. 'And do it now!'

Oswald's well-groomed appearance and the real interest he shows in the person with whom he is speaking gain him friends. Non-Christians are often drawn to him because of his intuitive understanding of what to talk about to them. And that has sometimes been a factor in helping to break down opposition from unsympathetic parents of young mission candidates.

But glib expressions of shallow religious thinking he cannot let go unchallenged. After Jimmy Carter had been elected to the American Presidency, a friend commented casually on how good it was to see a Christian in the White House. 'Yes, but is he a good President?' was his shrewd response.

And he can be quick to expose the fallacy behind would-be pious sentiment. A young missionary setting out from language school for his field of service arrived at the railway station to find that his train had already left. 'I think God must have meant me to miss that train!' he announced piously to accompanying friends. 'I think God must have meant you to know what time it left!' was Oswald's dry comment.

The suitcase that holds all his requirements for three or four months does not grow any lighter and he has no problem in identifying with the commercial traveller who pasted inside his suitcase the motto, 'God bless our home!' The path ahead must inevitably grow steeper, but while it remains open to him he goes steadily on, continuing, in the words of Edith's prayer for him, 'to make magnificent bouquets out of the refusals of God'.

19

Warts and All

Practically the only condition regarding the writing of this biography was that it must present a clear, full-face picture that did not attempt to smooth out the less attractive aspects of its subject – a 'warts and all' presentation. An honest attempt has been made, using all the resource material available, to present a thoroughly human, true-to-life picture. It has not been easy because, again to quote Dr Paul White, 'J O comes across as such a positive character.'

There are the obvious weaknesses of his strengths. A conscientious O M F home staff worker, who had to escort J O to an engagement, managed to get him there well before the scheduled time. Having to cross a big city in the morning rush hour, along an unfamiliar route, he had allowed for every possible contretemps, and not one had happened! So there they were outside the empty church with a good half hour to spare, while J O, his mind doubtless on urgent matters waiting on his desk, lectured his hapless chauffeur on the evils of wasting time! Nor did he leave it at that. 'Don't be too early!' he would say on future occasions. The unfortunate man was most apologetic about mentioning the incident, but it had clearly shaken him.

There was an occasion when he was chairman of the

Belgrave Heights Convention near Melbourne when Edith took her husband to task for changing arrangements for a morning prayer meeting at the Speakers' Lodge without regard for the convenience of the girls who had to prepare the rooms each day. It was only a small domestic matter, but Oswald knew that his genius for making snap decisions could sometimes have far-reaching consequences that he had not thought through in detail.

As a car driver he has not been highly rated, although he enjoys driving. It has been recalled that in Singapore he was booked about three times for exceeding the speed limit and the third time it was discovered that his licence had expired! He kept quiet about it at first, but finally in a somewhat embarrassed way he admitted that he was in trouble and had to appear in court on a charge of speeding and driving without a valid licence.

In general his brushes with traffic and other extraneous objects were of a very minor nature. There was a more serious occasion in Singapore when he was making a slow manoeuvre at a busy intersection without traffic lights. Suddenly a car travelling too fast from the other direction cannoned into the side of them. Oswald, his foot still on the accelerator, was knocked senseless. Mary was seated beside him, and only her calm reaction in taking over the steering wheel, while Michael Griffiths from the rear managed to switch off the ignition, saved them all from serious harm. As it was, Mary was found to have a broken collarbone, and both she and Oswald had broken ribs.

Ian Kemp, referring to Oswald's phenomenal capacity for hard work, hard travel, and a tight preaching schedule, tells of his arrival in India on one occasion, straight from a heavy programme of meetings in the USA:

Lumping a hefty brief case off the plane he walked into the airport eight hours late, having spent those hours sitting in the Bombay airport due to delayed flights. One would have thought he would arrive at the brink of exhaustion. But no, his walk was steady, and among his first words were notes of exuberance, 'You know, I had my eightieth birthday last Sunday. I was in Colorado Springs and spent it preaching twice to 5,000 people.' He talked all the way to Yavatmal (ninety miles in a car) and for five days fulfilled a heavy schedule of meetings ... One evening, before a packed chapel, I interviewed him for thirty-five minutes to extract information about his life and ministry. We then sang a hymn and I left him to it – he preached for an hour: clear, strong, relevant and full of the power of God. During those five days a few of his meetings were with only a dozen people around a conference table – but he gave his best to them as to the larger meetings.

He discovered that in Bombay someone had probably taken his passport, and that New Zealand had just closed its consulate, making it impossible for him to get a new passport in time for his scheduled return to New Zealand . . . but never did I see him perturbed – always quiet and confident. At the end of the five days I took him for further meetings with the diocese of the Church of North India in Nagpur City where he ate Indian food without any fuss and stayed with us in the NCC guest house, always obliging, never demanding, always accommodating. When only about fifteen very ordinary-looking pastors turned up for the pastors' conference in the NCC cathedral he proceeded with his ministry (by interpretation) as if it were to 5,000, believing God would use it for few or for many.

The account is so typical of Oswald's travelling ministry, and if one could hazard a guess at what he talked about during that ninety-mile drive, it probably centred a good deal around the interesting experiences of his recent North American tour. A few have felt this tendency to be something of a preoccupation with his own activities. But when Arnold Lea mentioned this trait he saw him as being 'the most unselfconscious person' of his acquaintance. The emphasis was always on amazement that God should give this ministry to *him*, of all people. And Dr John Laird was almost certainly referring to this when he said: 'There was something about him that I can only describe as modestly ingenuous.'

And so to sum up.

It is possible to read the earlier chapters of the Book of Genesis and to identify readily with Abraham, Isaac and Jacob. They embody so much of human frailty. Again and again they fall prey to the same temptations as are met with in the twentieth century. When Joseph appears on the scene he seems to represent a different league. It all seems larger than life, too good to be true. In this connection the Rev Derek Kidner has pointed out: 'The account of the dreams coming at the outset makes God, not Joseph, the "hero" of the story: *it is not a tale of human success but of divine sovereignty.*' (Italics mine)

It is equally possible to read the story of Oswald Sanders and to dismiss him as being 'out of our league'. To do so is to miss the fact that it, too, is essentially a story of divine sovereignty at work in the life of one man, shaping and preparing him for service. It is the story of a man who, from that moment at the Pounawea Convention, placed himself and all his concerns under God's control.

It is not only the story of what God could do with a man of exceptional gifts and above average energy and drive. Rather is it the story of what God can do with any life, at any level, no matter how ordinary it may seem, that is prepared to allow God to take the controls through all the checkered ways of life.

Again and again over the years, and particularly during the stressful years of OMF leadership, Oswald Sanders came to the place of saying: 'Lord, I can't take one more pressure!' But the pressures continued to come and he had learned to live by God's 'all grace' for every day and every circumstance. Results he left to the Great Shepherd; they were His concern.

'In his younger days I did not perceive Oswald Sanders to be a warm person: admirable, yes, but not warm. Nowadays I do perceive him to be a warm person.' That comment sums up much of the refining process in J O's life: the losses, the sorrows, the disappointed hopes, even the mistakes of a long life, have deepened his understanding and broadened his sympathies.

Where once he could be sharply censorious on matters of faith and belief that can divide sincere Christians, he can now be more accepting, while at the same time maintaining his own firmly-held views. As Leonard Buck said of him: 'He is an illustration of a man who has believed his beliefs and doubted his doubts and has gone on triumphantly with God. He hasn't gone on failing to face the realities of higher criticism and the philosophical areas that can keep men away from God, but he has gone on with God from strength to strength. And he has helped me to continue to continue.'

And that constitutes one good reason why so little has been forthcoming on the subject of 'warts'. Facets of his personality that may have been abrasive in earlier days have been smoothed out to insignificance over the years. As Michael Griffiths remarked: 'It is hard to remember that I ever thought him stern and austere. In later life the sheer warmth of the man is something I treasure greatly.'

He is still a quiet, shy man in most company, but has largely shed the tight, defensive cocoon, and has learned to cope with shyness in his own unruffled way. Wherever he goes he is no longer concerned to prove anything to himself or to anyone else. He is accepted just for himself and for what he is: J Oswald Sanders, man of God, speaker and writer, missionary statesman, servant of Christ.

Christ! I am Christ's! and let the name suffice you,
Ay, for me too He greatly has sufficed;

*   *   *

Yea, through life, death, through sorrow and through sinning
He shall suffice me, for He has sufficed:
Christ is the end, for Christ was the beginning,
Christ the beginning, for the end is Christ.

Saint Paul
F W H Myers